NO ESCAPE
FROM LIFE

Harper ▲ ChapelBooks

NO ESCAPE
FROM LIFE

by John Sutherland Bonnell

Harper ▲ ChapelBooks

Harper & Row, Publishers, New York

To my brother
DUNCAN JOHN BONNELL
whose example and encouragement
have ever been an inspiration to me

Contents

Foreword

This book has grown out of an experience of thirty years as a counselor. During that time more than eight thousand persons of diverse ages, from every segment of society, and with every type of human problem, have come to me for help. Some of these I have been unable to help; others have been led to a mastery of their problems. Every counselor learns much from those who come to him.

As a young man the opportunity was given me of two and a half years of psychiatric nursing in an institution for emotionally and mentally disturbed persons. Thus from the very beginning it was possible to bring to my work a sound psychological approach to those counseled and also to know when and where to refer those who needed specialized treatment or hospitalization. Later training for the Christian ministry revealed to me the limitless resources open to every man through faith in God. In circumstances where secular therapy has failed, the resources of religion have brought integration and healing.

A large church at the heart of the world's greatest city has provided a kind of laboratory of extraordinary opportunities in which to study human problems and to test the remedies these pages propose.

A line from A. Edward Newton says, "I wish that someone would give a course in how to live." It has seemed to me that during all my years of counseling I have been both pupil and teacher in such a course. All who came to my counseling room wanted to learn how to live more effectively.

Sometimes they came because of the negative drive to escape from life, and to find an "easy" way out of difficulty. Sometimes they came with the positive urge to seek resources to face life more effectively, and to master a discipline that would give daily help. What these persons brought with them and what we learned together about themselves, their strengths, weaknesses, and resources are reflected on every page of *No Escape From Life*. Obviously it could not have been written without their help. Together through the years we have been learning in the school of a master Teacher, using the world's best seller as a textbook, signed up for a course in how to live.

For helpful and faithful secretarial services, I am indebted to Mrs. Ronny Loucks, and especially to Mrs. Grace Schneider, my efficient manuscript secretary.

To my wife, Bessie Carruthers Bonnell, I am profoundly grateful for indispensable help. She has carefully read every page of the manuscript and ably assisted me with constructive criticism both of subject matter and English construction.

JOHN SUTHERLAND BONNELL

The Highlands
Prince Edward Island
September 15, 1957

1 Can You Stand Up to Life?

I remember the day Tom Dale walked into the counseling room of our church house. He was the very embodiment of defeat. He carried discouragement with him. It clung to him as a fog clings to a mountain. It was revealed in his drooping shoulders, slouching gait, a badly wrinkled suit, soiled linen, and a necktie that had slipped below his collar.

"I've got to admit that I'm a defeated man," he said. "I'm beaten. Life's got me down. You mightn't think it to look at me now but there was a time when I was a success. I even had a business of my own but that's all passed now. I've been out of work for six months and that's a pretty tough break for a man who has a wife and two young daughters to support. We've used up almost all our savings."

"Have you given your name to the agencies?" I asked.

"I did that months ago," he replied, "and I've had a half-dozen appointments but they just take a look at me and there's nothing doing. You'd hardly guess, Dr. Bonnell, that on one occasion in competition with sixty salesmen I got second prize. At that time I was selling automobiles. There was a business reorganization and I was let out. That knocked the heart out of me. For a while I sold vacuum cleaners but couldn't make a go of it. I tried insurance but that was an even bigger failure. I just seem to have lost my grip on things. I've lost my nerve and can't face life."

The interviews that followed disclosed that Tom Dale's father had died when Tom was a boy of ten. His mother, a former schoolteacher, returned to her profession. She devoted all of her hours outside the classroom to Tom, almost smothering him with affection, watching him carefully, guarding him from all kinds of dangers and possible illnesses, and shielding him from every reverse or discouragement. Strenuous sports were forbidden him because she feared he might be injured. If any trouble developed, she taught him to dodge it, to evade it, or to retreat from it. He did not marry until he was over thirty, his mother arranging most of the wedding details. Part of his personality was still a child attached to his mother. Emotionally he was dependent upon her. Now he was forty-three years old. The mother was retired but out of her savings and monthly pension check she managed to give him enough money to soften the blow of unemployment.

In additional interviews he told me of a recurrent dream, one that he had had almost as long as he could remember. It was concerned with difficulties in his past. A bear or a lion would threaten him, but always at the crucial moment when it appeared that he might be devoured by the beast, something would happen to deliver him. Sometimes a gigantic hand would reach down and lift him out of danger, or a fierce storm would arise, or darkness would descend—but always he was delivered without personal effort. Occasionally the dream took a second form of a landslide blocking his way, but just when he would decide to turn back a great bulldozer would come and clear the road for him so he could drive right ahead.

As we talked about these dreams he began to realize they were a reflection of his whole life pattern. He was always looking for someone to come to his rescue. This was also his attitude toward God. He often prayed that God would remove difficulties from his pathway, or that his mother or his mother's friends would help him out. Tom, up to this time, had been completely unable to face himself, to see his own "equation" written out.

After several months he took a moral inventory. He admitted one by one his various weaknesses and subterfuges, his devices for finding some means other than his own efforts to deliver him from difficulty and discouragement. He realized that his life pattern had to be altered, that he must learn to face life courageously. Instead of dodging difficulties or running away from them, he would have to meet them head on. He had to unlearn many of his mother's teachings. During one of the earlier interviews Tom said to me, "Before I came to see you, I was on the point of chucking all my responsibilities and running away. I had thought of going to another part of the country and starting life on my own."

Tom also began to recognize the immaturity of his religious ideas. He wanted God only in so far as he could use him. God was for him a kind of genie who, at his command, rushed to his rescue and delivered him out of danger and difficulty. Now Tom resumed his Bible reading, but this time for a totally different purpose. He no longer sought assurance that God would solve his problems and thus be a "cosmic servant." Instead, he sought to know God's will for him and how he might draw upon the divine strength in facing life bravely.

Before long, Tom Dale's favorite verse of Scripture was one found in the fourth chapter of Paul's letter to the Philippians:

"I can do all things through Christ who strengtheneth me"
(4:13).

He was impressed that the verse begins "*I* can do," and commented, "What I like about that verse is its emphasis on the
fact that we don't expect God to do everything for us. *I* can
do those things. *I* can face difficulties and obstacles in my pathway or the threat of danger. I can do them, but only because I
do them through Christ who strengthens me."

Months later Tom Dale told me he repeated these words whenever he met any discouragement or difficulty and they never
failed to renew his courage. They became a vital part of his life.
His new-found spiritual confidence affected every area of his
personality, his bearing, his manner of dressing, his attitude
toward life. At first he took a job that paid him only a modest
wage but which he felt was better than unemployment. He did
his job so well that one promotion followed another. At his own
church he joined a men's organization and shortly became head
usher. In the church a business executive was impressed with
his organization of the board of ushers. This led to a larger opportunity. Today he is in charge of the sales force of a large American business house. He said, "The stiffest battle I ever had was
to straighten out myself, to pull myself together, to get organized, to develop courage and faith so that I could stand up to
life." Back of every achievement he has made, he declares, is the
text that turned the tide for him: "I can do all things through
Christ who strengtheneth me."

In his book, *Psychology and Morals*,[1] the London psychologist
Dr. J. A. Hadfield writes, "When men are up against life and
find that it is too much for them, one swears, one gets a headache, one prays, and one gets drunk." He adds, "This is a statement of scientific fact." I suppose by that he means that it is a
true estimate of human life as it is lived today. People with far

[1] New York: Robert M. McBride & Co., 1933, p. 55.

less experience than he, in dealing with human problems, know the truth of this assertion. Innumerable tragedies result from the inability to face life bravely. Men fashion excuses to justify their failures. These alibis and rationalizations mark a well-beaten path. They are familiar to everyone who counsels people. "Life has been especially hard on me," says one. "I've never had a break," says another. "If only the good fortune that rests on other people would come to me even once, I could make a good showing too, but look at my situation." A third declares, "What can a fellow do who's got to face what is ahead of me?" One of the most devastating of all human attitudes is self-pity. It affords an excuse for our failures and is far from easy to overcome.

Often people fail because they have established a pattern of failure in life. From childhood they have never learned to face difficulties. When an obstacle looms up on life's horizon, they, like Tom Dale, begin to plan how they may evade it, how they can get around it, or how they may beat a hasty retreat. They refuse to face any kind of adversity. Their philosophy is set forth by Peer Gynt in Ibsen's play:

> To know for sure that other days
> remain beyond the day of battle,
> To know that ever in the rear
> a bridge for your retreat stands open.

Anyone who keeps his eye on that open bridge in the rear will never learn how to stand up to life.

ESCAPISM

The impulse to run away from life was so powerful in Tom Dale that he required many counseling sessions to reach the heart of his problem. The spirit of escapism, however, is in all of us. We have often heard people say, "I'm ready to leave it all." "I have a mind to throw the whole thing and quit." "I am fed up with this." Or, "I have had as much as I can take." And who of us has not at some time felt this way? If we should run away, however, even to the ends of the earth, we would carry most of our problems with us because they are a part of ourselves rather than of our environment.

The impulse to escape is certainly normal. The important thing is what we shall do about it. Shall we yield to this urge or will we have the strength of character to deal resolutely with it? There is nothing dishonorable in a desire to escape. It is wrong only when it becomes an obsession with us, when it begins to dominate our thinking. There are plenty of healthy and legitimate ways in which we may escape for a time from the pressure of our surroundings—a couple of hours at the theater, a night at the opera, viewing an absorbing motion picture, reading an interesting book, watching a ball game, or engaging in other forms of recreational activity. All of these pursuits will provide relief from excessive preoccupation with our daily routine. We all need an occasional break which, for a little while, will give us new and interesting surroundings, an opportunity to meet stimulating people and to engage in activities other than those that normally consume our time.

Thomas Carlyle says that the ultimate question posed by life is this: "Wilt thou be a hero or a coward?" How we shall answer this question will be determined by what we are deep within ourselves. Many modern people are attempting to run away from life by resorting to various forms of escape, the main ones being alcohol and the new tranquilizing drugs. The more extreme forms of escape are insanity and suicide. There is a common factor in these various modes of escape, especially alcohol, drugs, insanity, and suicide. All of them are symbolic of death, for death is the ultimate goal of all escapists who become enmeshed in their toils. Consider alcohol, for instance. The uncontrolled drinker is at peace only when he passes out. His end is death. On this subject Dr. David A. Stewart says,[2] "Escape and compensation are the chief goals of the alcoholic. He is not able to face reality. . . . *Alcoholism is a drive toward death* even though this may not be readily seen. The alcoholic is steadily approaching that goal and it is the sure end of the unresolved alcoholism."

In a later chapter on alcoholism this problem is dealt with at much greater length. It must be emphasized here, however, that the alcoholic drinks not because of his love of alcohol but because of the end which consciously or unconsciously he has in mind. That end is to escape from reality, to flee life. He accomplishes this, in a measure, by the illusory charm of alcohol which flatters his ego, making him feel self-important, calm, and relaxed. According to Dr. Stewart, "An alcoholic is anyone who drinks for the purpose of getting drunk."

The escapist under the influence of alcohol feels temporarily that not only can he handle his own problem with ease but that he can take on the whole world. Unable to deal with reality he flees into a world of fantasy where he can be what he wants to be *on his own terms.* But always there is the rude and painful awakening. Sobering up he must face the selfsame problems he ran away from, only now he is much less capable of dealing with them.

Many non-alcoholics drink not because of their enjoyment of liquor but because of the satisfying feelings it produces, the sense of well-being, poise and relaxation. Some people admit that when they go out with a group of their fellows, they are tongue-tied, self-conscious, and troubled by inferiority feelings until they have had a cocktail or two. One man of my acquaintance has often marveled at his increased ability as a conversationalist after having had a few drinks. Unfortunately, he has never had the opportunity under these circumstances to listen

[2] *The Drinking Pattern* (Campbellton, N. B.: Tribune Publishers, Ltd., 1951).

to himself! Otherwise he might arrive at a different judgment.
Dr. Abraham Myerson[3] writes:

> . . . there is a large group of those who find in alcohol a relief
> from the burden of their moods. . . . It deals out to them, temporarily,
> a new world with happier mood, lessened tension, and greater suc-
> cess. . . . Seeking relief from distressing thoughts and moods is per-
> haps one of the main causes of the narcotic habit. The feeling of
> inferiority, one of the most painful of mental conditions, is responsible
> for the use not only of alcohol but also of other drugs, such as cocaine,
> heroin, morphine, etc.

The sobering fact remains that such persons, if they are ever
going to learn how to live, must face reality without the aid of
alcohol or any other drug. There are constructive means of
getting rid of feelings of inferiority and depressing moods.
These must be sought and applied. The person who is determined
to engage in the pursuit of unreality often ends with the loss
of his job, his wife, his children, his home, his self-respect, his
hope, his confidence, and, unless the downward progress can
be arrested, life itself. One of the great challenges, therefore, is
to teach men and women how to stand up to life and meet
whatever it brings.

TRANQUILIZERS

In recent years a new menace has appeared on the scene in
the form of tranquilizers. Chief among these are chlorpromazine
and reserpine. They have the effect on the central nervous
system of reducing tension and anxiety and allowing people to
become more calm and relaxed. True tranquilizers require a
doctor's prescription. They are used widely today in the treatment of mental cases, especially schizophrenia. I have talked with
superintendents and medical staffs of a number of state mental
hospitals and they are unanimous in affirming that the use of

---

[3] *The Foundations of Personality* (Boston: Little, Brown & Co., 1931).

these drugs has greatly cut down the number of patients in these institutions. There were seven thousand fewer patients in mental hospitals in the United States at the close of 1956 than in the year before.

A second factor also has helped to reduce mental hospital population. State governments are now spending more money on their mental hospitals, the staffs have been increased, and consequently more time is given to individual patients. This matter of the time and attention devoted to each patient is a crucial factor in the patient's recovery.

Doctors are quick to point out that the tranquilizers themselves do not cure anything. They do quiet patients who are disturbed and excited, thereby preparing them to talk and to co-operate better with the psychiatrist who is trying to help them. Consequently, many thousands of them have been permitted to return to their own homes since the advent of tranquilizers.

The real problem presented to the American public is not from tranquilizers but from derivatives and new drugs containing tranquilizing ingredients. Unfortunately, these are purchasable without a medical prescription and for anyone so disposed there are thirty-one different tranquilizers to choose from. Most of the pharmaceutical manufacturers have a brand of their own. They differ slightly in chemical composition. In 1957 Congress appropriated two million dollars for the purpose of studying their effects.

Leading medical scientists are warning the public against a general use of these drugs. Very little is known about their toxic qualities and a great deal more research must be undertaken. In the meanwhile the Committee on Public Health of the New York Academy of Medicine's Sub-Committee on Tranquilizing Drugs recently made public the following statement: "In 1955 twelve cases of poisoning were associated with tranquilizers, seventy-six cases in the first ten and a half months of 1956, including two fatalities." No one knows the total amount of these drugs being sold without prescriptions. Unfortunately, many people who have been given these pills by doctors are distributing them among friends and relatives. This irresponsible behavior may do serious harm.

Here are considerations that should be kept in mind by anyone contemplating the use of tranquilizers in any form.

1. There are legitimate uses for tranquilizers, such as in the therapy of mental hospitals and by prescription under medical supervision.

2. The use of any form of tranquilizers without medical advice may be damaging to the person taking them.

3. It is necessary to increase the dosage from time to time to maintain the effectiveness of tranquilizers in easing tension. This has also been the experience with other drugs such as barbiturates.

4. Much emphasis has been placed on the fact that tranquilizers are not habit-forming. That may be true, but they will certainly be character-forming in that they will decrease the individual's ability to face difficult life situations. In other words, he will be psychologically conditioned to need them. He will be less able to face tensions and anxieties than he was before he resorted to tranquilizers.

5. The individual may forget that psychological tension is often a constructive element in life. The athlete who goes into a contest with no butterflies in his stomach and without perspiring hands is likely to lose. A certain amount of tension is necessary to the best performance of an artist, a surgeon, an athlete, a journalist, an editor, a court lawyer, a preacher, and many other professsionals. Cicero, the famous orator, never entered the Roman Senate to make one of his celebrated speeches without visibly trembling.

6. Tranquilizers may be a menace when used by drivers of automobiles. It has been demonstrated repeatedly in psychological laboratories that tranquilizers, especially those containing chlorpromazine, slow up psychological and motor reactions just as barbiturates do. They may temporarily disorganize the user's personality. They remove his anxieties and may relax his caution.

7. They do not induce sleep. They are not sleeping pills.

8. Placards in drugstore windows and other advertising urging the use of tranquilizers as a quick way to achieve peace of mind, and to eliminate worry, the jitters, and tensions, are misleading. These results may be achieved only at the cost of the individual's ultimate psychological and spiritual well-being.

9. It will be nothing short of a national disaster if these tranquilizers come into general use. Americans never do things by halves and there is danger of gross excesses at this vital point.

In the year 1936, Dr. Henry C. Link[4] said:

All the material advantages of our civilization conspire to make our lives easier and our characters weaker. Only the most intelligent and unselfish parents can counteract these harmful influences on their children. And only the sternest moral and religious convictions can safeguard the parents themselves from the easy manners of their environment. . . . The sins of the fathers' prosperity are visited upon the children and upon the children's children, even unto the third and fourth generation. The children of poor parents have a tremendous advantage in the struggle for character. . . .

These words are far more true today than they were when written two decades ago. With every year that passes the necessity for effort on our part is lessened. Multitudes are living today by the creed of comfort. We are producing a soft generation. Year by year new inventions make labor less and less necessary.

In some of his more recent lectures T. S. Eliot has warned that

[4] *The Return to Religion* (New York: The Macmillan Company), p. 178.

even in our pleasures we are eliminating all necessity for endurance or fatigue. The philosophy of life of many Americans is to achieve relief from every form of hardship. Little by little we are beginning to regard struggle, effort, and self-sacrifice as things to be avoided. We long for ever greater comfort. But our comforts do not make us happy. Distinguished visitors from India and other Eastern lands have marveled at the mental stress in American life—the surplus of tension and the evidence of mental and physical weariness.

It is hard to realize that many of these symptoms of mental stress have been produced by the lack of effort or exertion. Now at this critical juncture we have stumbled upon the tranquilizers so that it appears as though we can even rid our minds of their remaining anxieties. Our civilization may become akin to that of the lotus-eaters.

Many people are unaware that Aldous Huxley in his *Brave New World*—published in 1932—predicted the kind of existence toward which we are now headed, including an important place for tranquilizers. The brave new world would be one in which pain, struggle, discomfort, and effort would all be eliminated. Then just to make assurance doubly sure in case a little bit of irritation might creep into life, Huxley's world produced a drug called "soma" that took all the rough edges off life. This is how he describes it:

If by any chance something unpleasant should happen in this brave new world, there is always soma to give you a holiday from the facts. There is always soma to calm your anger, to reconcile you to your enemies, to make you patient and long-suffering. We carry our virtues about with us in a bottle. Christianity without tears—that is what soma is.

Near the close of the story a new character is introduced, a savage who has come from the outer fringes of that anemic civilization. He meets the controller of the world and the controller explains to him the nature of this society. At this point the savage breaks out in protest, saying, "But the tears are necessary. You get rid of them.—That's just like you. Getting rid of everything unpleasant instead of learning to put up with it, you just abolish the slings and arrows. It's too easy. I don't want comfort. I want God. I want poetry. I want real danger. I want freedom. I want goodness. . . ." When the controller assures the savage that he would be very unhappy in any other kind of civilization, the savage replies, "I claim the right to be unhappy."

One almost shudders to think of the disastrous possibilities facing us in America—the weakening of national character— if some of these tendencies should have their way. We are still in the midst of a cold war that gives every appearance of continuing. There are days of testing ahead for the American nation. Whether we wish it or not, we have been propelled into the position of leadership of the free nations of the world. Against us stands the colossus Russia—her peopl_ inured to hardship, trained and disciplined by austerity, ready to face difficulties. What chance would there be for us in any future struggle between the two vast systems that dominate the earth if the supreme tragedy happens and a third world war should descend on us? What hope of success would the American forces have if her soldiers, sailors and airmen went into the struggle fortified by their daily ration of tranquilizers?

SCHIZOPHRENIA

Habit patterns of retreat from difficulty and the non-medical use of alcohol and tranquilizing drugs are manifestations of escapism in American life. But so also are some forms of mental illness. This is especially true of schizophrenia. Dr. Leon J. Saul in his book *Emotional Maturity*[5] says that "schizophrenia means

[5] Philadelphia: J. B. Lippincott Co., 1947, p. 251.

not 'split personality' but a splitting off of the normal feelings and interests toward people and things in favor of preoccupation with one's own thoughts and fantasies." The beginnings of schizophrenia, at least the seeds of it, can be seen in children whose greatest enjoyment is found in solitary occupations. They have little pleasure in teamwork or games played with their fellows. They spend most of their time in daydreaming. They picture themselves as superman flying from planet to planet, a conquering hero at the head of a great army, a famous doctor or lawyer or preacher, but they do nothing constructive toward reaching these goals. Such daydreaming is hurtful when it is a substitute for actual achievement.

Similarly, the schizophrenic lives in his own private world of imaginings and distorted thinking. I remember well a patient twenty-two years of age who graduated with a B.A. degree from an accredited university. He was on my ward when I was an attendant nurse in a mental hospital. He would sit for four hours at a stretch without making a move and apparently unaware of the other patients milling around him. He had retreated to his private world. Like the daydreaming child, he was unable to face reality and the competitions of life in our society. This young student would become very angry at anyone who interrupted his reveries. He resented being asked to do even the simplest tasks because these pulled him back into the real world from which he was unconsciously endeavoring to escape.

A medical friend of mine tells me of one of his colleagues who had spent a year and a half in a mental hospital suffering from schizophrenia. After his release this physician went back to his practice. At the end of six months he told my medical friend, "You can never remotely imagine what a battle it has been for me to keep on with my daily task of seeing patients and helping them. Whenever a real difficulty intervenes, I look back longingly to my weeks and months in the mental hospital and recall how placid and serene life was there. Believe me, the pull back to that hospital ward is mighty strong. The temptation to run away from life again is at times almost irresistible." Here we have the doctor's afterthoughts on his mental illness. The original attack was of course involuntary and compulsive in nature.

A year or two ago a young woman, a sophomore student in college, came in for a series of interviews. Her first statement was this: "I had a nervous breakdown so I had to leave college." After four or five months of appointments I read back to her this statement. "Now," I said, "rephrase it to me on the strength of the insights you have gained." She replied quickly, "This is the way I would put it now: 'I had to leave college so I had a nervous breakdown.'" The transposition is revealing. The schizophrenic impulse is widespread today.

The Conditioned Reflex

When we meet life's complexities and difficulties, the one question of supreme importance is this: Do we possess adequate inner resources with which to deal with these situations? Can we face the worst that life has to offer us with an unbroken spirit? Few experiences have given to us a clearer realization of the necessity of such resources as the ordeal now known as brainwashing. This diabolically clever form of treating human beings has flourished for some years in countries behind the iron curtain. Probably the earliest manifestations of it came in the trials held in Russia during the purge that began in 1936. It was in Russia too that the philosophy behind brainwashing originated. Pavlov and his experiments demonstrated the conditioned reflex and provided the necessary ideas and know-how of the application of brainwashing to human beings.

Pavlov was not the first to write about conditioned reflex. As far back as the beginning of the seventeenth century, John

Locke demonstrated how likes and dislikes can be explained on the principle of association or conditioning. Locke pointed out that in the teaching of children this principle is constructively employed.

In 1890 William James wrote, "When two elementary brain processes have been active together or in immediate succession, one of them on recurring tends to propagate its excitement into the other." Here we have a principle very much akin to conditioning.

The great advance made by Pavlov lies in the fact that all his results with sensory stimuli and glandular responses were carefully measured and compared. He demonstrated the reality of conditioned reflex. This is the method that Pavlov followed: By means of a small incision an opening was made in a dog's cheek and a glass tube inserted. The saliva dripping from this tube was collected and measured in finely graduated containers. Precautions were taken that nothing would interfere with the dog to disturb him, so the experiments were carried on in windowless, soundproof rooms. The dog was fastened into a kind of harness and we are told that the animal was not uncomfortable during the experiment and actually looked forward to it, and would take its place on the operating table to have the harness adjusted.

While the dog was not aware of being observed, a bowl of food would be brought to him by a mechanical arm. As soon as this happened a bell would ring or a light would flash. As the hungry dog eyed the approaching food, saliva would begin to drip into the test tube. Each drop was counted and carefully measured. At first the dog was interested only in the food, and food alone produced the saliva. But occasionally an empty bowl would be presented to the canine and at such times the bell would not ring or the light flash. Every time food really appeared, the light would flash or the bell would ring and the saliva would appear. After a time the dog would hardly glance at the bowl but would wait for the light or the bell, and the moment the bell rang or the light bulb flashed, the saliva began to flow—the dog was now "conditioned." By the use of the term "conditioned" Pavlov meant a response that was induced by influence other than that of the dog's own native impulse. By "unconditioned" is meant, of course, the instinctive response of muscles like the involuntary blinking of an eye if somebody thrusts his finger near it.

There is good reason to believe that on Lenin's specific orders Pavlov extended his experiments to the Kremlin and that in that early day Lenin saw great possibilities for the use of this scientific instrument in the hands of the masters of Russia. Through systematic repetition and association, men could be trained to forget truth and affirm falsehood as automatically as Pavlov's dog had salivated at the sound of a bell.

The first inkling the free world had that some strange system was being employed by the Communists to obtain confessions came when observers saw one after the other of the old Bolsheviks enter the dock in Moscow and plead guilty of betraying the Bolshevism to which they had given their lives. They offered their testimony like men in a trance and many were the guesses in the press of the free world as to the procedure used to extort these confessions. Later, when these methods were used in Russia's satellites, we saw how even so able a man as Cardinal Mindzenty broke under the terrible brainwashing he endured. When he took his place on the witness stand and calmly admitted that he was guilty of many of the charges pressed against him by his prosecutors, the whole world gasped in amazement. Here seemed to be undeniable evidence that Moscow was right in the accusations it brought against these various political and religious leaders.

Not until the facts about brainwashing were brought out

following the Korean War was the nature of this horrible new instrument really known. It will be recalled that from Red prison camps in North Korea the voices of American and other Allied soldiers were heard admitting guilt for a whole series of different crimes and disowning their own countries. The voices were unmistakable, but listeners found it impossible to believe that these confessions and self-accusations could have been spoken by Americans. Now we know that they were and that these unbelievable admissions had been extorted by the brainwashing that came into existence through the application of Pavlov's principle of conditioned reflex. The governments of the United States, Britain, and other free countries that know the methods applied in brainwashing are now taking steps, in the training of recruits, to combat this menace.

It would be extremely helpful if all men entering the armed forces, all chaplains, clergymen, teachers, and others in leadership professions could read Edward Hunter's book on brainwashing.[6] Here he tells how certain men were able to resist the very worst that their enemies could do to them. It is highly significant that not only in Hunter's book but in books on brainwashing by other authors mention is repeatedly made of the necessity of religious convictions in combating this evil menace.

A dedicated Presbyterian missionary to China, the Reverend Dr. John D. Hayes, was one of those who demonstrated how invincible is the human spirit when it is reinforced with great religious convictions. Dr. Hayes was a son-in-law of the Reverend Dr. John Kelman, one of my predecessors in the ministry of The Fifth Avenue Presbyterian Church. When John Hayes returned to the United States, he visited our church and we learned at first hand some of the experiences through which he passed. Long before he was placed on trial, the process of

---

[6] *Brainwashing—The Story of Men Who Defied It* (New York: Farrar, Straus and Cudahy, 1956).

brainwashing had commenced. Then after his actual arrest and appearance before the Red tribunal, for forty successive days he was interrogated by relays of questioners for as long as nine hours a day. Even the slim diet given to Hayes at this time was measured with all the care that Pavlov measured the drops of saliva falling from the mouth of his dogs.

Every conceivable form of physical as well as mental pressure was exerted. The courtroom in which he was questioned was a room in the prison about twelve by eighteen feet in size. Here a succession of brainwashers worked on him daily. He was repeatedly charged with being an American spy and was assured that a full confession was the only way he could receive forgiveness. This man, born in China of missionary parents, said that his experience was like that of an operation being performed on his brain without the aid of anesthetics. The accusations made against him were repeated again and again and again, from every angle and by a whole battery of accusers, until the ideas were pounded into his brain. He used to exclaim, "If I could only have one square meal or one real night's sleep, I could stand anything." Even as it was, they did not succeed in breaking his spirit.

Hayes's knowledge of the Chinese language and of the Chinese modes of reasoning made him a redoubtable antagonist for the brainwashers. Day after day they attempted to becloud the mind of this remarkable missionary. So far had they succeeded that one night he suffered from hallucinations and appeared almost on the point of breaking up. They intended not only to break this man but to remake him in the communist pattern and use him against his own country. When the presiding judge continued to deny the truth of what he was saying, Hayes finally burst out, "All right, then, go ahead and shoot me, but I will still tell the truth." At that moment it was not the prisoner who broke but his judges.

Hayes himself repeatedly declared that it was his "crusading spirit," which had impelled him to become a missionary to the Chinese people, that made him eventually victorious. He said that from the beginning of his trial he had made up his mind not to win an argument against the judges but to try to make a friend of the enemy. His concentration on this point, impelled as it was by a great and unshakable faith in God, was the inner force that brought him through to victory.

An American soldier who also had survived the ordeal of brainwashing is quoted by Edward Hunter as saying, "What is most important of all is to have something in which you believe, some conviction about the dignity and worth of every human being, or an unshakable faith that there is a spiritual Power in the universe which we call God." These are the things that give a man strength to win through.

I vividly recall an address given by Robert A. Vogeler at the University Club, New York, a few months after his arrival in the United States. He had been in a Hungarian prison for eleven months. He declared that although he had never been much of a churchgoer, it was his faith in God and in the unique value of man that was the main source of his strength and of the resistance he offered to the enemy. One had only to look at his face and note the hesitation of his speech to realize how terrible was the ordeal that he had undergone.

I have dealt extensively with this subject of brainwashing because life itself can apply to human beings the principles of the conditioned reflex. The greatest assurance that we shall be able to stand up to life is that we have a definite purpose—the crusading spirit spoken of by Dr. Hayes. That spirit will keep us alive when there is every reason why we might welcome death as a relief from our troubles and difficulties.

SPIRITUAL RESOURCES

Professor Royce of Harvard said, "Faith is the discovery of a Reality that enables one to face anything that can happen to one in the universe." Can we have such a faith today? If so, how does it operate?

It begins with belief in God. By this we do not mean faith in a far-off infinite Intelligence that devised the universe, but rather trust in the God and Father to whom Jesus prayed. Now, we are free to deny such a faith if we choose. But few who do so have the courage to face the implications of their own skepticism.

Nietzsche was one of the few men in history who, having rejected God, faced the consequences of his decision. He knew that the denial of God was not simply the denial of a holy and loving Guardian of our lives. The German philosopher carried his "sad lantern" down all the corridors of human life until he had denied everything having purpose, order, or meaning in the universe. Finally he completed the syllogism of his logic by going mad.

Some of Nietzsche's views were put into practice by the Nazi government of Germany, and the leaders of Nazism adopted them as a personal creed. We know what this destructive philosophy brought to the world in widespread devastation and indescribable loss of human life. But what did it do to the individuals who accepted it as a personal creed?

One of the notable books written since the close of World War II is a little work entitled *The Last Days of Hitler* by the English author H. R. Trevor-Roper. He was an intelligence officer of the British Army. Trevor-Roper describes the happenings in the Bunker under the Chancellery in the weeks before Hitler's death. When it became abundantly clear that the complete collapse of the Nazi regime was rapidly approaching, Hitler arranged a last dinner with his chief lieutenants and their wives. Four of the women were present. Goebbels was there, too, but not Frau Goebbels. She shared her husband's atheistic creed. Why, then, was she not present at this farewell dinner? It was true that she had accepted her husband's skepti-

cism but she shrank back from its terrible, logical denoue-
ment. Trevor-Roper reports in cold, measured words: "Unnerved
by the approaching death of her children, she remained all day
in her room." According to the plan, on the day following
Hitler's death Goebbels and his wife poisoned their six children
before themselves embracing death, and Frau Goebbels could
not partake of that final meal with the realization of what the
morrow was going to bring. The Nazi-atheistic creed had come
full circle—"The slow sure doom falls pitiless and dark."

One thinks of the words of Paul describing the plight of the
pagans of his day, "Having no hope, and without God in the
world" (Eph. 2:12).

Perhaps the best way to judge one's own convictions is to
examine resolutely the alternatives to them.

How does faith in God enable one "to stand up against anything that can happen to one in the universe"? Because such a
faith gives meaning to life as well as direction and purpose. It
gives us something enduring to live by. When everything around
us is cracking and sagging and giving way, it undergirds us with
unyielding foundations.

An illustration of the spirit of escapism is found in the 55th
Psalm. The Psalmist wants to run away from life. He writes,
"Oh that I had wings like a dove! for then would I fly away,
and be at rest." The author of this psalm is said to have been
King David, although this cannot be proved. However, David
fits very well into this situation. He had good reason for want-
ing to flee from Jerusalem. There was grave trouble in his kingdom. His own son had raised the standard of rebellion against
him. Instead of loyalty and love, he greeted him with hatred.
Lawlessness and violence were running riot in the streets of his
capital city. As he brooded on his troubles, he became panic-
stricken. His heart was rent with anguish. Fear and trembling
overwhelmed him. "Uneasy lies the head that wears a crown."

And King David had plenty of reason for uneasiness. Looking back in later days upon this dreadful experience, he declares somewhat apologetically, "And I said, Oh that I had wings like a dove! for then would I fly away, and be at rest."

"Well, David, if you had wings, where would you fly?"

"I would wander far off, and remain in the wilderness."

What wilderness is he talking of? Those rocky hills beyond Bethlehem where as a lad he watched his father Jesse's sheep. He had often seen dawn rise over these mountains. Far off the blue-capped peaks stood like sentinels by day, and at night the stars came out to keep him company—and in all that solitude he never knew a lonely moment, for God seemed always near.

David wanted to get back to his childhood again. Actually the essence of schizophrenia is regression to childhood. For all of us childhood is a symbol of the comfort and protection of our parents, and all the carefree hours seem, in memory, to have been filled with innocent joys.

> Backward, flow backward, O tide of the years!
> I am so weary of toil and of tears—
> Toil without recompense, tears all in vain—
> Take them and give me my childhood again![7]

It is so easy to forget that childhood too had its toils and its tears.

Yes, some of the best-known characters of the Bible at times were almost overwhelmed by discouragement and were ready to quit. Elijah, valiant-hearted man though he was, became utterly panicky in the face of the enemy and fled off to the wilderness. Cowering under a juniper bush, he prayed, "It is enough; now, O Lord, take away my life; for I am not better than my fathers" (I Kings 19:4).

Jeremiah, made sick at heart by the sins of his people and oppressed by life's burdens, cried, "Oh that I had in the wilder-

[7] Elizabeth Akers Allen, "Rock Me to Sleep."

ness a lodging place of wayfaring men; that I might leave my people, and go from them!" (Jer. 9:2).

And Paul, a towering figure among the apostles, in a moment of discouragement declared, "I have a desire to depart, and to be with Christ; which is far better" (Phil. 1:23).

Who of us has not wished for "wings like a dove," or Elijah's "juniper bush," or Jeremiah's "lodge in the wilderness." For the city dweller of today the modern equivalent of these is "a cabin in a northern woods" or "an island in the southern seas" or "a shack high up on a lonely mountain."

One day a New York bus driver became wearied of impatient passengers and demanding schedules. Not having "wings like a dove" with which to get away, he took the next best means and disappeared with his bus and wasn't found until he had journeyed some 1,500 mlies south of New York. There were lots of people who understood exactly how he felt. And wasn't it only a short time ago that New Yorkers were snapping up real estate shares on the moon? They were really going to "get away from it all."

Consider again the words of the Psalmist, "Oh that I had wings like a dove! for then would I fly away, and be at rest." David believed for the moment that rest is a matter of location, that it is a geographic point. But it is not. Rest is a state, a disposition, a mood of the soul. It is not to be found in a specific locality. A dove, when it is released, flies in wide circles to get its bearings, and then goes off swiftly in a straight line to its destination.

If you had wings like a dove and decided to use them to fly to the uttermost part of the earth, to what land of peace and security would you fly? Where would you find the lotus-eaters' paradise where you could dream away your days? Remember this—if you ever did find it, you would carry with you your deepest source of discontent—yourself. So Milton writes,

> The mind is its own place, and in itself
> Can make a heaven of hell, a hell of heaven.

That was what David discovered, so he didn't run away. He mastered the desire to flee all life's unpleasantness. The very next day he was back in the struggle again and this time won out.

Later in the same chapter he writes, "As for me, I will call upon God; and the Lord shall save me. . . . He hath delivered my soul in peace from the battle that was against me." God's help came to him in the midst of the battle, not in running away from it. He finally saw that what he needed was not wings to fly with but firm feet to stand on, a brave heart, and patient endurance.

"Do not pray for easy lives," said Phillips Brooks. "Pray to be stronger men. Do not pray for tasks equal to your powers. Pray for powers equal to your tasks."

One of the most popular sports writers in Britain prior to World War II was Geoffrey Gilbey of the *London Daily Express*. His numerous friends were shocked to learn that he had suffered a shattering nervous breakdown. He went to the seaside and returned somewhat restored. Then followed a second breakdown and a third. He tried to explain them by overwork, by the stress of his surroundings, by the inconsiderateness of a few friends, but all the while he knew that these were but empty excuses, that the true explanation would be found deep within himself in some dark schism within his own soul. He was unable to face life. Out of the abyss into which he had sunk, he cried to God for help. Stretching forth a hand of faith into the night that enveloped him, he felt an answering touch. God was indeed there, a living reality, and Gilbey was strengthened and restored. In gratitude for the new life welling up within him, he wrote a little book entitled *Pass It On*,[8] a book that has brought hope and reassurance to thousands.

[8] London: Hodder and Stoughton, 1950.

Geoffrey Gilbey made a discovery which people are slow to perceive, that most nervous breakdowns are caused, not by our environment, but by something amiss deep within ourselves. The surroundings or environment provided the occasion, but not the cause, of the personal failure. Naturally, the reference here is not to an acute psychotic condition over which the individual has no control.

During the Civil War Nathaniel Hawthorne once confessed, "The present, the immediate, and the actual have proved too potent for me." Yes, and the present, the immediate, and the actual are proving too much for many a person in our own time.

These stressful and grim days in which we live are testing the moral and spiritual mettle of multitudes. Modern man may be likened to Goethe's Faust. His restless mind is probing the secrets of the universe. He has advanced in science and philosophy, but in so doing has pledged his own tormented soul and discovered that he has made a sorry bargain.

The only adequate answer to the demands of modern life is spiritual resources. We are accustomed to see in the windows of banks and trust companies a notice saying that the reserves are so many million dollars. The institution is assuring us that even though our economy should pass through a stormy and testing time its reserves are adequate to meet the crisis.

But far more important for the happiness and well-being of the race are moral and spiritual reserves. Home and family life are today being subjected to extraordinary tensions, and a disturbingly large percentage of homes are breaking up. What they lack is a reserve of love and affection to fall back upon. The individual too is under pressure. We all know the heartbreaking shocks that are the lot of many men and women. Perhaps it is a business reverse, or a sudden unemployment, or a medical verdict that changes the whole outlook of the future, or a crushing bereavement that blots the sun out of the sky and turns day into darkness. Human lives are being stretched and pressed to the breaking point in our time. So a poet sings:

> If every man's internal care
> Were written on his brow,
> How many would our pity share,
> Who have our envy now![9]

But where and how shall we find the interior resources with which to stand up to life? St. Paul answers that question in these words: "May the Lord of peace himself grant you peace continually, whatever comes" (2 Thess. 3:16). There are at least two kinds of peace: first, there is the peace of passivity, the peace of unbroken calm, of exemption and negation. How well I recall an instance of such peace—a pond set in the heart of a swamp. It was always a dread place in my childhood, a spot to be shunned. Its placid waters were covered with a green scum and were never disturbed by even a solitary ripple. Over it hung a deadly calm, like a miasma. There was something sinister about it. It savoured of rottenness and death. That is the peace of passivity.

The peace of which the apostle speaks is the second type— an active and dynamic peace, one which can exist amid troubled circumstances and keep us inwardly strong. You will note that he speaks of it as "peace continually, whatever comes"; in sorrow as in joy, in storm as in calm. It is the gift of the Lord of peace. He did not promise his disciples exemption from life's trials. He offered them no immunity. On the contrary, he predicted distresses and troubles. There are today some sects on the fringes of Christianity that promise freedom from the hardships of life if one follows their creed. It was not so with Jesus. He said, "In the world ye shall have tribulation," and that word "tribulation" is from the Latin meaning a flail. He said, "You will be beaten by the flail of adversity." But then he added

[9] Pietro Metastasio, *Giuseppe Riconosciuto*.

triumphantly, "Be of good cheer for I have overcome the world." In his strength we too shall win the victory.

The Psalmist writes, "The Lord is on my side; I will not fear: what can man do unto me?" (118:6). The fear of man, of any man, no matter how great or powerful, vanishes when we are garrisoned by such a faith and possessed by such a peace.

Jesus is called the Lord of peace; so he is, for his every word and action breathe forth inner serenity. It has been truly said that Jesus was always in command of himself and of every situation whether it was a father urging him to hasten to a dying child, or the madman of Gadara descending to the shore with disheveled hair and wild, staring eyes, or a raging storm on the Sea of Galilee, or the howling mob at Jerusalem, or the trial before the tribunal of the Roman Procurator, Pontius Pilate. In every situation Jesus was calm and untroubled. Yes, he is in truth the Lord of peace. His own explanation of this inner strength and quietude is that daily and hourly he was in contact with God.

It is almost unbelievable that we too may have a daily encounter with God, that each of us can maintain "a silent sanctuary" within his breast. We can commune with God as we walk down a crowded street, as we ride in a bus, as we enter a store or carry on our duties in office or factory or school. We can turn to God at any moment and even those who are closest to us cannot hear the closing of the door as we enter a secret oratory and are inwardly renewed. Then peace will abide in our hearts, peace that begins at the center of life and reaches out to its circumference. Then there will be no undue strain or tension, no fuss or feverishness, no wasteful anxiety. We shall have the strength to face life with courage.

The person who has convictions and draws upon the resources of the Christian faith can face the stresses and strains of life without quailing. He will meet trouble courageously and will never run away from difficulties. He will refuse to indulge in self-pity. He will neither whine nor complain. He will not become bitter or rebellious. Instead he will draw upon limitless resources of courage and faith that will enable him to stand up to life.

Further consideration of available spiritual resources must await the last chapter. I should like, however, to include here the story of a young woman who was a member of a group in our church that was formed so that its members might share with one another the helpful messages they had received from their daily reading of the Scriptures. Each member of the group makes a note of what he has found most helpful in his reading. Sometimes these verses result in dramatic happenings that are told at the next meeting of the group. By fellowship and sharing of spiritual resources every member of the group is inwardly strengthened.

At one meeting, a young woman who had had a difficult battle with alcoholism told of this incident: One morning she was on her way to a television studio and called a taxi. As they proceeded, the driver leaned back in his seat and said to his passenger, "New York is a hell of a city to be living in. Everybody is at everybody else's throat. The competition is killing. It's confusion worst confounded."

The young woman said, "I don't blame you, driver, for feeling that way. I used to think like that myself a while ago."

"Why don't you think that way now?" he asked.

"Well," she replied, "I have made a discovery that has given me the strength to be able to 'take' New York."

The driver glanced back suspiciously. "What do you mean? Now don't start telling me that you got religion."

"I don't care how you describe it," she said, "but I have something deep within me that keeps me calm and untroubled even in New York."

"What have you got?" he asked her.

She answered, "Each day I read in my Bible where I left off the previous day. I read on until I get a verse that offers help for the new day. This I copy out and carry with me. I find it inspiring."

"Did you get a verse this morning?" he asked with increasing interest.

"Yes, I did," she said. "Now that I think of it, it seems to have been sent for you more than for me."

"Well, let me hear it anyway," he remarked.

She reached into her purse, took out a slip of paper, and just before reading it, she said, "You spoke of New York being confusion worst confounded. Listen to this: 'God is not the author of confusion, but of peace.'" (1 Cor. 14:33).

"Let me see that thing," said the driver as he reached back for the slip of paper.

He held it in his right hand as it rested against the wheel and every now and then glanced at it. When they reached their destination, she paid him and then passed him a tip. He brushed it aside, saying, "Lady, I couldn't take a tip from you. You have given me something this morning that is more important than all the tips I'll collect today."

If we are to remain steadfast in our allegiance to the highest, like this young woman we shall daily require inner renewal. The Bible is an unfailing reservoir of spiritual power. At this source we may constantly "renew our strength." All this is true not merely for day-by-day living but also for those testing times when we meet life's crises and the very foundations are cracking and sagging under our feet. Then we shall need to look beyond human resources to find strength for the ordeal, for in such an hour man's help is often vain.

Seldom has this truth been so graphically illustrated as in the life of Edward Sheldon, the well-known playwright. His biography, *The Man Who Lived Twice*,[10] has gripped and inspired the American people. Rendered completely immobile by a crippling form of arthritis, which in its later stages also left him totally blind, Sheldon manifested extraordinary courage and faith which enabled him to triumph over his affliction. After the onset of this disease he wrote to his friend Van Wyck Brooks, "I never felt the need of a definite religion until recently. I used to think I could stand up to anything that came along, but I don't any more. . . ." Sheldon's biographer then adds these illuminating words:

During the next weeks he came to grips with destiny and from some hidden reservoir of the spirit drew strength to go on. He not only found the courage to endure under a blight from which death might have seemed a welcome release, but he formed the sure belief that affliction could not destroy the purpose of his life. . . . in the moment of crisis he found a faith which would not only sustain him in the thirty remaining years of his life but which would reach out in powerful and mysterious ways into the lives of other people.

What lifted Edward Sheldon above his fellows was his discovery of this "hidden reservoir" of spiritual power that enabled him to face with serenity and courage whatever life might bring.

[10] By Eric Wollencott Barnes (New York: Charles Scribner's Sons, 1956).

2 Anxiety—the Disease of Our Age

A young woman eighteen years of age came to see me with a problem of intense anxiety. She was personable and attractively dressed.

She said, "I live in a home of five children with my mother and father. There are two boys and two girls besides me. I happen to be the youngest in the family. My problem centers in my inability to be at ease in the presence of young men. My mother and father have given me every encouragement to date boys and have welcomed them into our home when they come. I seem to get along all right with them until they show some seriousness about our relationship. If a boy shows a tendency to go steady and even remotely hints of a later possible engagement, I am thrown into emotional turmoil. My hands perspire and I start to tremble, and I get him out of the house as fast as possible. No other member of our family seems to have this trouble. One of my sisters and both of my brothers are married and the other sister at home is engaged. The whole situation troubles my father and mother very much.

"There is another aspect of this situation that puzzles me. I made application a little while ago to be admitted to a parochial hospital near our home, submitted all the necessary papers and was accepted as a future probationer. The moment I was accepted I became terribly nervous and went to the superintendent of the hospital and withdrew my application. This has happened three separate times. The pastor of my church called me in and asked me about it. I told him that I didn't feel well and strong enough to undertake the duties of nursing. He said, 'Well, you look strong enough to me. Is there something else the matter?' Why should I act like that? What rhyme or reason is there to that kind of behavior? My parents were very much put out over it all. There is a young man who has come to our home to see me on several occasions and now he wants us to become engaged. I have been offering all kinds of excuses about why I can't date him and on one occasion when he came to the house, I hid. The family couldn't find me and said I must have gone out. I was trembling with fear."

The young woman could give no clue whatsoever as to why she went into these states of acute anxiety. During the course of interviews we repeatedly went back to her early memories but nothing that seemed particularly relevant to the situation was uncovered. I noticed, however, that in the period from the age of five to six there seemed to be a severe blocking of her memories. All her dreams also were dreams of fear. Sometimes she dreamed of a man chasing her with a knife in his hand. It became obvious that her condition of anxiety was due to some severe psychic shock she received in childhood. Then one day the story came out. She told it with great difficulty and trembled visibly as she talked. She couldn't tell me the story directly. I had to ask question after question to elicit the full information.

It appears that when she was in her fifth year she had received a very severe fright because of a male exhibitionist who lived some four or five blocks from her home. I had to ask such questions as, What time of day did it happen? Was it on the street or in the home? Was it on the doorstep? How old did the man seem to be? et cetera. Bit by bit in great agitation she unfolded the story. Not satisfied with exposing himself to the child, he ran down the steps toward her as if to catch her. She fled crying bitterly. When she got near her own home, she stopped and dried her eyes and checked her sobbing. When she went home she told nobody of the episode and had never shared it with anyone until the day she unfolded it in the counseling room of our church house. So overcome was she with emotion when she had finished telling her story, that she had to rest for almost an hour before leaving for home.

Little by little she gained insight and understanding of her problem.

"I see now," she said, "how this wretched fear has worked its way right into the very center of my life and why I am afraid of young men and shy away from engagement or marriage."

Shortly after this I asked her to explain to me why she had rejected the nursing appointment. For a moment or two she was puzzled and then her face lighted up and she answered, "I can see it all now. I suppose it was because unconsciously I realized that in the course of my nursing duties I would have to wait on men and the old fear blocked me at this point too."

This case history reveals the intense power of a repressed fear in producing anxiety that manifests itself in later years.

Still another case in which an adult fear apparently grew out of doubts and inferiorities experienced in childhood, is the story of a businessman thirty-nine years of age whom we shall call Ben. He came to talk to me about his troubles with his business associates and his deep sense of insecurity. He had been transferred from a South Carolina town to take charge of the sales force in his firm's New York office. Formerly he always enjoyed his work and had been remarkably successful. Now it had become an almost intolerable strain for him to go to his office. He was impatient and overly exacting with his salesmen so that two of the best men on his staff had left for work with another firm. The general manager had complained that there was a loss of efficiency in the sales staff, that a competing firm was taking over some of their customers, and that the sales manager's own results had become increasingly unsatisfactory. Ben said it was always a severe ordeal when he had to go into the general manager's office. He avoided contact with him whenever possible. He said it was even a task for him to pass by the desks of his own salesmen on his way to his inner office.

In the last few days before his visit to me new symptoms of disorder had appeared. Now he found it hard to ride on a bus or a subway. He was experiencing a growing dislike of people. He was tired of the crowds and if anybody jostled him in the bus, he would break out in some expression of irritation. Looking at me with entreaty in his eyes, he said, "Something has to be done and done quickly, or I shall be permanently sunk."

It was not surprising to learn that matters had become very difficult for his wife and his two children. Ben was unbearably exacting with the children and when his wife interceded in their behalf, he would get angry at her.

"I am afraid all the time," said this businessman. "Fear is my constant companion every hour of the day. It keeps me awake at night so that I can get to sleep only with the aid of barbiturates. Each morning as I wake I am full of foreboding. Fear meets me at my bedside when I get up and it never leaves me throughout the day."

It was quite obvious that this was no instance of ordinary fears that could be banished by some magic formula or a

couple of interviews. We all meet with normal fears that are
an inevitable part of life itself. They are intertwined with the
very business of living and, as will be shown later, we have to
build within ourselves sufficient internal resources to deal with
them.

In Ben's case, there was a mingling of normal fears with
neurotic anxieties because now he felt that he was caught like
a rat in a trap. While I planned to have him in for a series
of interviews, I knew also that he would require immediate
help to get by in his day-by-day task. As an immediate measure
I suggested that he quit going back to his office on Sundays,
which he told me he had been doing, and that he spend his week-
ends with his family and renew his church attendance.

Additional interviews revealed that while new and heavier
responsibilities in more tense surroundings had somewhat overwhelmed him, it was also true that his present inadequacies were
linked with childhood inferiorities and fears. One interesting
discovery was that the general manager of his business organization reminded him very much of his own father in appearance
and manner. His father had dominated him right up to young
manhood and was severe in all his dealings with him. From
childhood, too, he had manifested a sense of inferiority and an
expectation of failure whenever major difficulties presented
themselves. He was at his worst, so far as effectiveness was
concerned, when he found himself in new and strange surroundings.

Ben came to see that the only way he could overcome his
fears and anxieties was to develop goals, values, and resources
mightier than the evils that threatened him. I reminded him of
the words of Elisha to the young man who was his servant.
"Fear not: for they that be with us are more than they that be
with them" (II Kings 6:16).

Ben discovered that faith in God promotes courage and trust,
that trust fosters love, and that love enables him to live more

serenely with others. The spirit of love enabled him to forgive those persons against whom he had taken a dislike and who he felt had injured him. Gradually he learned that "divine resources available through prayer and worship" were not just words a preacher might use, but practical, down-to-earth help.

Near the close of the series of interviews he said to me, "My spiritual experience can be summed up in a verse I found in the 34th Psalm. 'I sought the Lord, and he heard me, and delivered me from all my fears.'

"Oh, I know," he added, "there will be inner rumblings from time to time of some of those anxieties that had their origin in childhood, but now I know them for what they are and with the help of God I will never let them enslave me again."

As Ben re-established a closer relationship with God, little by little he began to realize God's love for him and the Heavenly Father's care of him and his wife and children. Day by day this realization made it a little easier for him to love people, even beyond his immediate circle of family and friends. As he rode on the subway or bus, for example, he picked out certain individuals and prayed for them. Usually he would select persons who seemed distressed or overburdened with the cares of life and he prayed that God would give them strength for the tasks of the day and enable them to face life courageously. He said that this silent prayer for the people around him brought a distinct change in his attitude toward them. The more he prayed for these people, the more friendly he felt toward them. The change, he said, was remarkable. He undertook also to learn something about the home life of the salesmen who worked under him—whether they were married or single, how many children they had, what their circumstances were. His interest in these men very shortly brought a change in their attitude toward him as well as in his feelings toward them. Instead of tension, resentment, and fear dominating the life of this business office, understanding, good will, and co-operation now prevail.

Not only has he found the more abundant life for himself but day by day he is bringing it to others.

NORMAL AND ABNORMAL FEAR

The words "fear" and "anxiety" were both used in describing the two cases at the beginning of this chapter. As used in common parlance the words are often misunderstood. They have separate and distinct meanings. Fear means emotional agitation because of a specific danger which threatens. Anxiety, which denotes a more serious condition, means the presence of a deep-rooted concern, the object of which is unrecognized. When we are anxious, we are not only fearful, but also apprehensive, uneasy, and yet not able to tell why we are so full of foreboding.

Dr. Karen Horney, the psychoanalyst, distinguishes between fear and anxiety by saying, "Fear is a reaction that is proportionate to a danger that one has to face; whereas anxiety is a disproportionate reaction or even a reaction to an imaginary danger."

Before discussing anxiety further it might be helpful to consider fear in both its normal and abnormal aspects.

In the opening paragraphs of his book, *The Conquest of Fear*,[1] Basil King writes: "During most of my conscious life I have been a prey to fear ... I cannot remember the time when a dread of one kind or another was not in the air." Thousands of people could truthfully echo his words. Fear is one of the greatest scourges of the human race. It is universally present. A helpless little babe may be afraid even when yet

> An infant crying in the night;
> An infant crying for the light;
> And with no language but a cry.[2]

---

[1] Garden City, N. Y.: Doubleday & Co., Inc., 1921, p. 1.
[2] Tennyson, "In Memoriam."

Psychologists, by means of laboratory tests, have established that at birth two fears are already present: fear of a loud noise and fear of falling. One morning in a New York hospital a probationer entered the nursery carrying a tray of bottles. She made a misstep and suddenly the whole load crashed to the floor. Instantly a score of babies began to cry bitterly. They were manifesting one of the two innate fears—the fear of a loud noise.

That day a minister was visiting a sick parishioner in another part of the hospital. His parishioner was ninety-three years of age. Looking at the minister with dread in his eyes, he said, "I find that I am daily growing weaker. The end can't be far off now, but I am afraid to die." Thus from the very beginning of life to its close fear is an implacable enemy of man.

In earlier years it had been assumed that children are naturally afraid of the dark, of strangers, and of animals. But such childhood fears are not innate. Professor John B. Watson conducted an extensive series of laboratory experiments with babies between the ages of four months and a year. It was found that these little ones had none of these fears unless they had been taught them by grown-ups. When furry animals were introduced to the children, they immediately reached for them. One eight-month-old baby tried to stuff a rabbit's ear into his mouth. Of course, that is the baby's way of getting acquainted with things. The experimenters even took the babies to a zoo. They were shown lions, elephants, and other animals. None manifested a trace of fear. One little boy wanted very much to stroke a tiger!

While we begin our lives with only two fears, it is not long before we succeed in accumulating scores of additional ones. The fear of thunder and lightning, of the dark, of people, of life, and of death—these have all been taught to children by adults, or they have learned them by watching adult behavior.

Inappropriate anxieties arising within the individual are not based on reality. The disproportionate reaction comes when people are afraid to walk on the streets, afraid to cross a street, afraid to ride in automobiles, on trains, or in airplanes. A natural fear has become unnatural and destructive. And as for the imaginary fear, tens of thousands of people throughout this nation are afraid every time they open a letter, tremble when they see the telegraph boy, are startled when the telephone rings or even when someone suddenly calls to them. They live in constant fear and feel that some strange, indefinable menace haunts all their days.

But fear may be helpful and constructive. Were it not for normal fear, thousands of lives would be lost through carelessness. Who of us would be willing to trust himself to an airplane pilot who knew nothing at all of fear? Who would be willing to accept medicines compounded by a pharmacist completely lacking in a sense of responsibility? The fear of making an error keeps such men alert and scrupulously careful in their work. In hundreds of ways fear is thus a safeguarding factor in human society. Nevertheless, when a constructive fear has been exaggerated out of all proportion, it may become destructive. It is normal to have a dread of want, and it may lead to industry and thrift, but when this fear is greatly overexaggerated, it may transform a man into a miser, like the man from Illinois who had $300,000 in cash and securities hidden about his house and yet starved to death in the midst of this wealth. It is normal to fear a speeding motor car. When, however, a teen-age boy visibly trembles while crossing the street, something more than normal fear is evidenced. Common sense dictates that one should wash his hands with soap and water before eating. This is a sensible precaution against bacteria, but on one occasion I talked with a woman whose hands were cracked and the skin broken and bleeding because a hundred times a day she washed them in strong disinfectant. This compulsive washing was beyond the power of her will to control and was due, probably, to a deep-rooted sense of guilt. A constructive fear had become an anxiety. George Eliot says, "It is well that fear should sit as the guardian of the soul, else how should man learn to revere the right?" Abnormal fear, however, causes uneasiness, tension, and loss of self-confidence.

> The thing that numbs the heart is this
> That men cannot devise
> Some scheme of life to banish fear
> That lurks in most men's eyes.[3]

But a scheme of life *has* been devised that will banish abnormal fear. It is set forth in the pages of the Bible. It is not possible to expel from the mind negative, destructive, unwholesome thoughts merely by an act of the will. It is useless to say, "I will not let my mind dwell on these things." They will return to plague and haunt despite the best of resolutions. There is only one way in which an undesirable, negative thought can be driven out, and that is by the substitution of a powerful, positive thought, what Professor William James of Harvard called "the expulsive power of a new affection."

A creative, dynamic, spiritual force, such as faith in God, possesses the power to expel the destructive emotions preying upon mind and heart. This statement is likely to be discounted because it is made by a clergyman, but the same affirmation is made by many medical scientists. Dr. William S. Sadler, the Chicago psychiatrist, writes, "The only known cure for fear is faith."

True Christian faith does not say to us, "Don't be afraid. The thing that you fear will never happen. The tragedies that happen to other people will pass you by." On the contrary, the faith of Christ teaches us to say, "No matter what mis-

[3] James Norman Hall. Used by permission of *The Atlantic Monthly*.

fortunes come my way, I will look them in the face. I will
meet them one by one and demonstrate that they are not to be
feared."

During the course of World War II, I spoke often to American soldiers who had finished their preliminary training and
were awaiting embarkation overseas. In every instance I reminded these young men that they would know the meaning
of fear—when they boarded transports for overseas, when zig-
zagging at night through the U-boat zone, when they landed
on foreign shores with a ruthless and desperate enemy awaiting
them—and that this was normal and natural. They were helped
most, I found, by a statement that I repeated in every address:
"Courage is not the absence of fear; it is the mastery of it. We
are cowards only when we permit fear to dominate and control
us." On each occasion I gave them one verse of Scripture to
hold in their minds: "I will fear no evil, for thou [God] art
with me." On parade grounds, in army hospitals, and in military prisons men have repeated these words with me in unison.
As Joanna Baillie says:

> The brave man is not he who feels no fear,
> For that were stupid and irrational;
> But he, whose noble soul its fear subdues,
> And bravely dares the danger nature shrinks from.

In Britain during World War II land mines were sometimes
dropped by the enemy—long cylinders of steel attached to huge
silken parachutes. One night there was a severe raid. At day-
break a warden was horrified to see a mine hanging from a
steel girder and swaying in the breeze. He called for the demoli-
tion squad. A thirty-foot ladder was placed against the girder,
and a young officer in khaki ordered all his men away. He
climbed up to where the deadly mine was hanging and examined
it carefully to ascertain whether or not it contained an inner
fuse that would explode a few seconds after the outer one had

been removed. After a painstaking inspection he took a wrench and slowly and carefully began to remove the fuse. The mine, finally rendered harmless, was lowered to the ground. A friend said to the young lieutenant, "I take my hat off to you. How you can do that kind of thing without being afraid, I can't understand."

"You are mistaken," the officer replied. "Every time I am called to one of these jobs, I am afraid, but I master my fears. I must, because if my hand trembled on the wrench, that moment would probably be my last."

"Would you mind telling me how you master your fears?" he was asked.

The lieutenant hesitated, and then smiling shyly, replied, "Well, it goes back to my childhood in Scotland. I have never forgotten a Bible verse which my mother taught me: 'Yea, though I walk through the valley of the shadow of death, I will fear no evil: for thou art with me' [Ps. 23:4]. I have been down in that valley many times, but on such occasions I am able to master my fears for I believe that God is with me and nothing else really matters."

ANXIETY: CAUSES AND CURES

As I have emphasized earlier, anxiety is a term that is more inclusive than the word fear. Anxiety is also more harmful and should be dealt with in the context of this discussion of escaping from life's realities, for anxiety is a negative form of escape. When we allow our minds to dwell upon conscious or unconscious worries and forebodings, we are failing to live creatively amid the concerns and opportunities that the present hour provides.

To understand our anxieties we should question what causes them and see possible ways in which they may be dealt with constructively. I suggest five causes of widespread uneasiness, the first one being *economic anxiety*. It is true we are living in an era of prosperity, a time of abundance, but many people still carry with them the scars of the great depression, and they continue to live under its shadow. But even now millions of Americans are harassed constantly by economic strain. The minister of a Presbyterian church located in the suburban area of one of our great cities said to me recently, "You would be amazed to know how many of the families in my church live close to a financial precipice. They are mostly younger people and they feel that they must have every gadget, every convenience, every luxury that their neighbors possess. They are pledged to the hilt with future payments and as a consequence they are always anxious."

Modern advertisers have done their work so well and have employed psychology so skillfully that, for instance, people are almost ashamed to admit that they don't possess a television or hi-fi set, an electric dishwasher or an up-to-date automobile. The confession is made apologetically, "But we are planning to get one soon." The pressure toward conformity is powerful in our land. Too many people have never learned to understand the words of Jesus that "a man's life consisteth not in the abundance of the things which he possesses" (Luke 12:15). The words of the Hebrew prophet have a present-day application: "You have sown much, and harvested little; you eat . . . but you never have your fill; you clothe yourselves, but no one is warm; and he who earns wages earns wages to put them into a bag with holes" (Hag. 1:6, RSV).

What shall we say of the mad scramble for wealth today, for social position, prestige, and power? Always the Bible brings its penetrating answer: "Give me neither poverty nor riches; feed me with the food that is needful for me, lest I be full, and deny thee, and say, 'Who is the Lord?' or lest I be poor, and steal, and profane the name of my God" (Prov. 30:8, 9, RSV).

Jesus saw clearly that economic anxiety blinds men to the truth that "man shall not live by bread alone, but by every word that proceedeth out of the mouth of God" (Matt. 4:4). Our Lord's final judgment on the subject of our possessions is, Put God first. Give him priority. "Seek first his kingdom and his righteousness, and all these things shall be yours as well" (Matt. 6:33, RSV). That's the only dependable cure for economic anxiety.

A second type of anxiety is the anxiety of worry. Jesus said, "Do not be anxious about tomorrow" (Matt. 6:34, RSV). Are these the words of an impractical dreamer? Do they suggest an ideal impossible of fulfillment in our Western world? Jesus lived in a small country. He journeyed by foot from place to place. He dressed in the simple garb suited to a warm climate. He was not required to meet the heavy expenses that fall to us in educating a family. He did not face the burden of an extensive correspondence or the complexities of modern life. Food, heat, and shelter presented problems quite different from those of our time. Jesus did not have to meet the exacting demands of parental responsibility. One might ask: "Why shouldn't Jesus say 'Be not therefore anxious for the morrow'? What did he have to worry him?"

It is true, of course, that the social and economic life of Jesus' day was simpler and more primitive than ours, yet plenty of people had anxieties. Life for them was just as difficult as it is for us. They had to struggle to maintain their humble level of existence.

Were food and clothing matters of indifference to Jesus? New Testament scholars believe that Joseph, the head of the home, died when the Master was but a youth. The burden of supporting a widowed mother and six or seven little children fell upon his young shoulders. It was no light matter, in ancient Nazareth, to provide food, clothing, and shelter for the little brood of a Galilean carpenter. The parables of Jesus give us glimpses of his family life. He told of women grinding wheat with the primitive stones of that early period; of the housewife putting leaven into the meal; of a little boy asking his father for bread, or for an egg, or for a bit of fish. These were the cheapest foods available in Palestine. He tells of a thrifty mother patching old garments, or searching diligently for one small coin that has been lost. Who can doubt that in some of these parables we have a portrayal of Mary, his widowed mother? We gain insight too into those early years through the words of Jesus spoken during his ministry: "They that are gorgeously appareled dwell in kings' houses."

It must indeed have been a severe struggle for our Lord and his mother to keep the little home together. It may be that these early responsibilities proved a clue to the long delay in the commencement of his lifework. He was thirty years of age when at the Jordan he dedicated himself to his God-appointed ministry. In the light of all the facts how significant are his words: "Be not therefore anxious for the morrow."

The King James Version translates these words as follows: "Take therefore no thought for the morrow." One commentator refers to this as "a most unfortunate mistranslation." It is not a mistranslation. It is perfectly accurate seventeenth-century English. "Take thought" means to be troubled or to be anxious. One sees this in Shakespeare's play *Julius Caesar*. The dramatist makes Brutus say of Mark Antony: "If he love Caesar, all that he can do is to himself, take thought and die for Caesar." In other words, "Yield to melancholy brooding and pine away for Caesar." "Take therefore no thought for the morrow" means "Do not be anxious or troubled about the morrow."

The words "Take no thought" in their former connotation would seem to indicate that Jesus commended or encouraged improvidence. He never did that. Improvident people are a burden to others. He did speak of the birds that "sow not, neither do they reap nor gather into barns," but the birds are not improvident. Watch them. See how carefully they construct their nests in anticipation of a little family. When the eggs are hatched, they search diligently for food to sustain their young. In the economy of nature many creatures lay in store the food that will serve them in bitter days of need. While it is true that their behavior is largely instinctive, it is poles removed from improvidence.

Jesus planned carefully for the future. He deliberately ordered the entire course of his ministry, including his return to Jerusalem and the cross. He planned the selection of the twelve disciples and the sending out of the seventy on an evangelistic tour. He organized all the details of the Last Supper, and, prior to that, the triumphal journey into Jerusalem. The disciples had their own small treasury for emergency needs, though most of it was distributed to the poor. If Jesus were living in any great city today, he would still say, "Be not therefore anxious about the morrow."

There is a vast difference between legitimate planning and senseless worry. We of the Western world need to take to heart the admonition of Jesus regarding anxiety, for it is a major scourge of our time. An eminent British physician, Dr. C. W. Saleeby, has called it "the disease of the age." We are an anxious, careworn, fretful generation.

Never before has this land been so rich in labor-saving devices and material comforts. Yet with every increase in these devices comes an increase of worry and anxiety about the future. We worry also about episodes in the past that cannot be altered, and about happenings in the future that may never occur.

"God grant me the serenity to accept the things I cannot

change; the courage to change the things I can and the wisdom to know the difference." These are wise words. Two things nobody ought to worry about. One of them is the things we can change. It is stupid to fret about matters that we can alter. Let us get busy and change them. Why should we wring our hands about conditions in our land or in our home or in our personal lives that can be changed? Let us change them.

We should not worry about circumstances that we cannot change. We must learn to accept them, to admit their reality, but we need not let them crush us. God will give us strength and courage to master the unavoidable.

In the course of World War II, I visited the home of a dear friend, a fellow minister, who had just received word that his only son had been killed in the Battle of the Bulge. This boy had decided for the Christian ministry and possessed excellent qualifications for that vocation. His father was brokenhearted. As I sat with him in the comradeship of silence, he began at last to talk very tenderly and lovingly about his boy. Then he said this: "I am not going to be bitter or rebellious. He is gone. Some day I hope to meet him again. One thing I will say: I must now be twice as good a minister as I have ever been because my son will not be here. I shall try to do his work as well as my own." He faced the inevitable bravely and robbed it of its power to destroy him.

If we shouldn't worry about the things that can be changed and the things that cannot be changed, what then is left to worry about? Let us summarize the lessons the Master teaches us.

Live one day at a time. Leave the past and the future in the hands of God. Forget the failures of the past and the fears of the future. Do the best you can today. Live one day at a time.

Some years ago a physician gave me a copy of *A Way of Life,* a little book by Sir William Osler, who was a distinguished medical scientist in three nations—Canada, the United States, and Britain. It contains an address he had given to the students of Yale University. This was his message: "If the load of tomorrow be added to that of yesterday and carried today, it will make the strongest falter." Live in day-tight compartments. Don't let yesterday and tomorrow intrude on your life. In other words, live one day at a time. "Then," said Dr. Osler, "you will avoid the waste of energy, the mental distress, the nervous worries that dog the steps of the man who is anxious about the future." Live one day at a time.

Are there moral failures in the past? Then, in the spirit of contrition, commit them into the hands of a loving and forgiving God who says, "I, even I, am he that blotteth out thy transgressions . . . and I will not remember thy sins" (Isa. 43:25).

Is there unhappiness in the past? Don't brood about it. Don't let it poison your soul. Don't go on the treadmill saying, "If I had done this or if I had done that or if I had done the other thing, it would all have been different." That is the way to nervous disability and mental breakdown. Entrust all these things to God. He will give you power to rise above past unhappiness.

Is it anxieties regarding the future that worry you? Recall the words of wisdom uttered by Balzac, the nineteenth-century French author: "After all, our worst misfortunes never happen and most miseries lie in anticipation."

Live today. There are people who just couldn't keep on living if they thought of the days ahead but they have found strength to live one day at a time. That is all that God asks of any of us.

A well-known American novelist said that one day as he stepped into the kitchen after supper and stood watching his wife washing dishes, he thought to himself, "If that poor woman could just look ahead and see the dishes that will remain to be washed in the future towering like a mountain, she would give up right away." Then he reflected, "But she has only to wash today's dishes."

There is homely wisdom in that thought. Live one day at a time.

Another way to avoid the anxiety of worry, which not only the words but the example of Jesus teaches us, is to *do something for somebody else every day,* an unsolicited kindness, a word of encouragement and hope spoken in another's hour of need.

Worry springs largely from self-centeredness. How much better to follow the motto of Edward Everett Hale:

> To look up and not down,
> To look forward and not back,
> To look out and not in,—
>   and
> To lend a hand.

The greatest worrier I have ever known is one who possesses every comfort and luxury that money can buy but lives in an ever-present atmosphere of depression and gloom. George Bernard Shaw, speaking of a certain character, says that he was "a self-centered little clod of ailments and grievances, complaining that the world would not devote itself to making him happy."

Do something for somebody else, for at least one person, every day and it will minister the grace of God to your soul. Even the uttermost in tragedy can be turned to victory through unselfish service to others. Happy people are helpful people.

Finally, *trust God.* This is the remedy that Jesus offers for worry. Worry always reveals unbelief—a lack of trust and confidence in God. It prevents us from enjoying God's good gifts that are already ours and even from realizing their presence.

"Be not therefore anxious for the morrow." The word "therefore" in this text refers to the Heavenly Father's unfailing care of which our Lord has been speaking. This does not mean that he promises us an escape from the troubles of life. None of us knows at what moment the blow may fall. The Christian faith is not a dugout in which we may hide. It is not a "safety-first"; it is not an escape from life. It is rather the means of triumphing in the hour of adversity through trust in God our Heavenly Father.

In Emerson's *Journal* is a tender passage regarding his little boy Waldo who had died. Emerson was resting in the woods. He was sitting in a natural armchair made by the upturned root of a pine tree. In that moment his thoughts were on his boy. Then imperceptibly he began to feel the healing power of the universe around him. Later he wrote, "All that I have seen teaches me to trust the Creator for all that I have not seen." That is a sound philosophy and is in full accord with Jesus' teaching. He says, "Trust in God." Leave the unseen future which troubles you so much in the hands of God.

Thomas Guthrie, one of Scotland's greatest preachers, was once making a journey to another parish. He traveled by boat, by coach, by railway. All the while he was accompanied by his little four-year-old boy. They were constantly seeing strange people and new sights. Through it all, he said, the little fellow did not manifest the least anxiety. Dr. Guthrie began to ask himself why. Suddenly he realized that all the while the little boy's hand was in his father's and so he was unafraid.

Are you worried about yourself, your health, your inner weaknesses, your future? Are you worried about financial matters, about loved ones who are ill? Are you worried about our world and what may happen to it?

Live one day at a time. That will be enough. Plan for the future. Prepare for the future. But don't worry about the future. Do the best you can each day for yourself, for your fellow man, and for God and leave the future to him. Reach out a hand of faith and put it into your Heavenly Father's hand and you will cease to be anxious. With him beside you, you cannot fail.

The third anxiety causing widespread suffering is based on fears of an atomic and hydrogen holocaust.

On August 6, 1945, an American bomber took off from little Tinian Island in the Pacific Ocean and headed for Japan. A few hours later a parachute fluttered down over the city of Hiroshima. Suddenly there was a blinding flash of light accompanied by a terrific explosion. More than 78,000 persons were killed, more than 37,000 injured, and more than 13,000 missing when this first atomic bomb was exploded over that great city. When this news broke upon the world, the American people were themselves stunned and bewildered. We possessed, we were told by the scientists, a weapon of unparalleled power that would make us invulnerable to attack so long as we were the sole possessors of it. From that moment fear began to grip the hearts of the American people. We, who possessed the atomic bomb, were more afraid than anyone else.

In the years since then every additional increase of atomic destructiveness has added to our concern. Would other nations hostile to us discover the secret? How many years' advance have we over them? Will our stock pile be larger than theirs?

While the menace of atomic warfare is far greater than it was five to seven years ago, the general public feels that the potential destructiveness of hydrogen weapons has become so great that the major powers will not risk the mutual annihilation of a third world war. Nevertheless, an atomic anxiety hangs over the nations like a sword of Damocles.

One reason this anxiety has become universal is because of the advance made in communications. The loneliest outposts of the world are in touch with day-by-day happenings in the centers of civilization. In America, with radio, television, and successive editions of the newspaper, a continuous impact is made on our minds by world events. We go to bed at night with the last radio bulletin informing us that Russia has exploded another hydrogen device and we wake in the morning to read in the headlines that a new crisis is developing between East and West.

Thus for the first time in history we are witnessing anxiety on a global scale. It is sweeping across every continent of the world and all the islands of the oceans. It spreads like an epidemic and is equally contagious. In the fourteenth century the Black Plague devastated Europe. In London carts were driven through the streets at night with the drivers ringing a bell and calling, "Bring out your dead! Bring out your dead!" The present epidemic of anxiety throughout the world has produced far more casualties than the Black Plague, even if its results are not always as fatal.

In the Gospel of St. Luke our Lord tells of an era when there shall be wars and commotions, nation rising against nation, kingdom against kingdom, earthquakes, famines, pestilence, religious persecution, and "men's hearts failing them for fear and for looking after those things which are coming on the earth." For us who live in this atomic age these words have a strangely familiar sound. Whatever interpretation we may give of Jesus' eschatology, this at least is sure: he never doubted the final victory and vindication of God's eternal purposes for his children. He always saw light on even the blackest horizons of history. What then has the Master to say of the mood in which we are to meet these critical times? In striking contrast to the hopelessness of many advocates of stoical cynicism today, he said, "When these things begin to come to pass, then look up, and lift up your heads; for your redemption draweth nigh" (Luke 21:28).

The Christian faith promises no immunity from the storms and testing experiences of life, but it keeps us calm and resolute in the midst of them. In fact, we are to expect difficulties and test-ings and know that our faith grows when, in the words of Robert Browning, we

> . . . welcome each rebuff
> That turns earth's smoothness rough,
> Each sting that bids nor sit nor stand but go!

Even though universal destruction should threaten to sweep across the world, true believers in God will remain undismayed, for they know that the values they cherish are indestructible and that nothing can separate them from the love of God or pluck them out of the Heavenly Father's hand.

David E. Lilienthal, one of our greatest authorities on the atomic bomb, says, "Our security rests not on material things but on the spirit of the people. When we substitute for this faith in weapons, we become lost."

Futhermore, it is idle to think that we can run away from our atomic fears by finding an imaginary refuge, a safe hiding place. Edith Wharton, in *A Backward Glance,* retells an ancient tale of the city of Damascus. One day when the sultan was in his palace, a beautiful youth, who was his favorite, rushed into his presence crying in great agitation that he must flee at once to Baghdad. He implored his majesty's leave to borrow his swiftest horse. The sultan asked why he was in such haste to go to Baghdad. "Because" the youth answered, "as I passed through the garden of the palace just now, Death was standing there, and when he saw me, he stretched out his arms as if to threaten me. I must lose no time in escaping from him."

The youth was given leave to take the sultan's horse and flee. When he was gone, the sultan indignantly went down into the garden and found Death still there. "How dare you make threatening gestures at my favorite!" he cried.

Death, astonished, answered, "I assure your majesty I did not threaten him. I only threw up my arms in surprise at seeing him here because I have an appointment with him tonight in Baghdad."

When our post of duty is at Damascus, it is utter folly to flee to Baghdad. That ancient tale has its counterpart in modern life.

In May, 1789, while the Connecticut legislature was meeting, the sky was suddenly and fearfully darkened at noon. A strange and awesome twilight fell over all the land. Many people were filled with terror believing that the end of the world had come. The lawgivers trembled beneath their legislative robes. One arose and said, "It is the Lord's great day. Let us adjourn." Then rose Abraham Davenport, who said in the words of John Greenleaf Whittier's stirring poem,

> Be it so or not, I only know
> My present duty, and my Lord's command
> To occupy till He comes.
> Where He hath set me in His providence
> I choose for one to meet Him face to face
> No faithless servant frightened from his task.

And so the candles were lighted and the legislature continued in session. The poet concludes,

> And there he stands in memory to this day
> Erect, self-poised, a rugged face half seen
> Against the background of unnatural light
> A witness to the ages as they pass
> That simple duty hath no place for fear.

The prophet Isaiah uttered challenging and inspiring words when he said to his people, "Strengthen ye the weak hands, and confirm the feeble knees. Say to them that are of a fearful heart, Be strong, fear not" (Isa. 35:3, 4). The man who has truly committed his life to God in complete surrender can stand erect in the face of "unnatural light." He can say with the Psalmist, "The Lord is on my side; I will not fear: what can man do unto me?" (Ps. 118:6), and with Paul, "If God be for us, who can be against us?" (Rom. 8:31).

As always, we are brought back to the towering figure of the Great Physician, whose life was a constant manifestation of the power of faith. "He was always in command of himself and of every situation. He was never embarrassed or taken by surprise, always poised and self-possessed. He was never in haste, never anxious, never jealous or impatient with anyone."[4] As he moved among men and women exercising his ministry of redemption and healing, he brought to them unfailingly a sense of God's presence and power.

In the hour when he stood on trial for his life with the populace clamoring for his crucifixion, he was the only person in that judgment hall who was completely unafraid. The people were afraid of their Roman rulers; the soldiers were afraid of their superiors and the iron hand of Roman discipline; Pilate was afraid of the displeasure of the Emperor. Only Jesus was completely devoid of fear, for he could say, "I am not alone, for my Father is with me."

A fourth cause of anxiety is seen in the attitude of some persons toward grief. Most people have more difficulty with grief than with any other problem. Every observant person is aware of the fact that when bereavement visits a home, every member of the family is tested to the core of his being. Whether or not we can handle grief is determined largely by the measure of faith we possess and also by our understanding of the problems that sorrow raises.

Let us look at some of the unconstructive ways that people meet grief. There are, of course, right and wrong ways of dealing with it. One of the most serious mistakes we can make is to refuse to express our grief, to keep it bottled up or, as some

[4] Karl Ruf Stolz, *The Church and Psychotherapy* (Nashville and New York: Abingdon Press, 1943), p. 64.

people express it, "to keep a stiff upper lip," to refuse to admit even to ourselves that we have suffered a crushing loss. It is a totally wrong idea that we ought to be stoical and completely unemotional in the face of death. Nature should be allowed to have its way. The Lord gave to us lachrymal glands that we may use them, and the flow of tears is healing to the spirit.

Another unconstructive response to grief is the development of feelings of guilt. These are almost inseparable from death. Rarely do I find anyone who has suffered a grievous loss in death who does not express some guilt: wondering if the loved one had been sent to the right hospital, if the proper doctor had been engaged, if all the needed attention had been offered, with many expressions of regret for unkindness or thoughtlessness or lack of sympathy with the one who has departed. A measure of this is normal and natural but when it becomes obsessive, it can be dangerous.

Overactivity is another response that may have harmful results. Tennyson, after the death of his friend, Arthur Hallam, declared, "I must lose myself in action, lest I wither in despair." Activity of a constructive nature is quite important and beneficial but when it is just a matter of constant hurrying and bustling in unimportant matters, it is an evidence of grief that has been repressed, that has not been allowed expression.

All three of these reactions were manifested in the life of Mrs. James who was referred to me by her doctor. She told me that her son had been killed in the Korean War. The word was late in reaching her. She had not even known that he would shortly be in action, and it was a terrific shock. She said that now she had to be a "soldier" too. That in itself was quite a proper resolve, but she interpreted it as a demand to repress every sign of sorrow. She was moody, restive, irritable. She had developed symptoms of physical illness for which her doctor could find no physiological basis. The grief that she refused to admit was expressing itself in other ways that were harmful and destructive. When I talked with her husband, he told me that she had become very difficult to live with. Formerly she had been a most co-operative and affectionate person. He said, "The death of our son seems to have changed her nature." Quite unconsciously, she was also expressing hostility for the dead boy because he had not taken a college course that might have kept him out of the army. She was unaware, of course, of this hostility but her husband was now bearing the brunt of it. She also had troublesome feelings of guilt lest she had not sufficiently urged her boy to go to college, that she had not written to him often enough when he was in training camps in America and in Korea, or she hadn't taken enough care of him or given him sufficient instructions on safety measures before he left.

In the matter of purposeless activity, she was again manifesting her repressed grief. She was carrying too heavy a load of social responsibilities, especially with patriotic societies and also with her church. She was always urging the minister to find her more work to do yet was at the breaking point because of inner tension that was never relaxed and a load of unceasing duties.

My first task with this woman was to persuade her to recognize the death of her son, to admit it to herself and to others, to let her grief have its way, to shed tears for the sorrow that had come to her and her husband. It was very difficult to achieve this end and I succeeded only by asking her many questions about the boy, about his earlier years, about her care of him, about his schooldays, about his expressions of affection. She brought me letters that he had written from Korea and as she read these to me, for the first time tears began to flow. I talked to her about feelings of grief-guilt and explained how a pilot of a plane returning from a bombing mission would sometimes be incapacitated by guilt because some of his crew had been killed by shrapnel.[5]

Little by little she began to see that these feelings of guilt were a normal reaction to bereavement, but that it was useless to feel guilty for situations in which she had no responsibility. Her overactivity was corrected when we worked out a schedule of helpful services in a veterans' hospital near her home. She saw the foolishness of many of the pointless activities in which she was engaged and gradually eliminated them. She continued one or two simple church duties and her visits to the veterans' hospital. The time came when she was a great comfort in that institution and was known to most of the boys as an understanding and helpful person.

One of the important factors in her recovery was her faith. Previously, after she had learned of her son's death, she had taken all his civilian clothes and had them dry-cleaned and hung in his closet ready for use. She said, "Everything must be there to remind me of him. It would be disloyalty if I let myself forget him for a moment." When she really accepted the Christian teaching that life goes on beyond death, that death is not a blind alley but an open road into new and adventurous experiences with new opportunities of service and worship in the Heavenly Kingdom, she began to talk of the spiritual progress that her son would be making in the new life. Her rekindled faith in God and in the world to come led her to part with all her son's clothing, sending it to boys of needy families.

She received great comfort from the words of a poem which she kept before her on her writing desk:

> My knowledge of that life is small,
> The eye of faith is dim;

[5] For additional information on this theme see R. Grinker and John P. Spiegel, *Men Under Stress.*

But 'tis enough that Christ knows all,
And I shall be with him.[6]

A year or two ago on my *Pilgrimage* radio program over WABC and its network I used, in dramatic form, this story of the boy killed in Korea and told how his mother overcame her persistent grief by admitting to herself the death of the boy and drawing upon the resources of the Christian faith. Soon afterward I received a letter from a radio listener. She stated that both she and her husband had received great help from that broadcast on grief. She added that a few years earlier her teenage daughter had been killed in an automobile accident. She was on her way to Florida with two other young women of her own age. They were all killed. The girl's father had been ill ever since this tragedy, for his life was wrapped up in his child. Her room had been left exactly as it was, with all her athletic equipment, her banners, her Sunday School mementos, records of her Young People's work and many honors and awards she had received. The bereaved couple had read books together, which helped a little, but soon they would find themselves back again in the depths of their sorrow. Friends tried to help but lost patience with them and as a consequence they were estranged from many people. The daughter's desk in her room had been quite undisturbed, with her writing paper, pens and everything else intact.

"Your radio program on grief," she said, "greatly encouraged us and enabled us to understand why we have reacted as we have toward our dear girl's death. Now God is giving us the strength to deal resolutely with this situation. We have made changes in our daughter's room and will continue to do so just as the mother did of whom you spoke in your broadcast. Little by little we shall dispose of her clothing where it will do the most good. I will close this letter," she added, "by telling you

[6] Richard Baxter.

that I am using this beautiful blue stationery taken from my daughter's desk as evidence of the fact that we have changed our former attitude toward our bereavement. This writing paper has never been touched since she left us, so you see that, through the story of another mother, God has moved in a mysterious way his wonders to perform."[7]

Some people deep in their bereavement will only require certain facts about grief to be brought to their attention. Their own insights will teach them the best thing to do, and, as always, their faith in God and in the eternal life which he has promised to his children will be their strength and stay.

Another incident sheds further light on the subect of the anxiety of grief. A young doctor brought his wife to my office. They did not come to discuss a problem of grief. They were concerned with the fact that their marriage had become very insecure. They had two children—a boy and girl both under five years of age.

"There is something wrong with our marriage and there always has been," the doctor said. "I love my wife very dearly and I hope she loves me, but there seems to be some barrier in her life that keeps her from entering wholeheartedly into our marriage. She seems to build up a wall against me. Our marriage has never been really happy either physically or spiritually. I am hoping that there is something you can tell us that will help to change this situation."

At this point his young wife broke down and cried bitterly. She said, "I know I don't love my husband as I ought to. I try

[7] Recently while addressing a group of ministers in a neighboring state, I was led to tell this story, fresh in my mind, having written it out for this chapter. At the close of the meeting one of the younger ministers came to me and said, "I know that woman of whom you have been speaking. It may interest you to know that in addition to her good works you have referred to, she has established a scholarship for divinity students in memory of her daughter. I am the first recipient of a generous annual gift from this fund. Without it I might not have been here today."

to but something holds me back."

That morning we set up a counseling program for both husband and wife but principally for the young wife and mother. After five or six interviews she recalled many memories of her childhood. They were all closely associated with her father. She was the youngest child and hence the apple of his eye. The two older children were boys. He used to take her on his knee and caress her. She was, as he put it, "just my little girl." The moment he entered the home she would fly into his arms and climb on his knees. Often at the dinner table she would sit on his lap. When she was eight years of age the father suddenly died. His daughter was away at the time visiting a relative and they didn't ask her to come home until after the funeral. When she found that her father was no longer there, she was utterly inconsolable. They told her that he had died, but she had never experienced death in the family or among friends and the word meant nothing to her. Of only one thing was she sure—her father had suddenly gone. She was completely lost and brokenhearted. Often she would go to her mother and attempt to sit on her mother's knee, but the mother was too busy with the cares of the household and would push her off, saying, "You're too big a girl to be sitting on my knee." Time and again she was repulsed by her mother.

About two years later the mother remarried and a stepfather came into the home. When the mother told her about the new father she had high hopes that she would now receive some of the love she had had from her own father. Her hopes were bitterly disappointed. The stepfather had no interest in her whatsoever. In fact, he barely tolerated her. All through her teens and in college she kept before her the mental image of her father—as though he were alive. She had a feeling that he was somewhere in the world and she would yet find him. This was true even when she became engaged and married and after the birth of her children.

It was obvious that she couldn't give herself completely to her husband because her father was still her first love. She felt that loyalty and devotion to him demanded that everybody else in her life would have a secondary place. This fact she would have to see and understand for herself; not only had she to grasp it intellectually but it had to penetrate into her feelings. She had to know in her deepest being that her father had died and that in her lifetime she would never see him again.

As we talked about death and its meaning and of the unconstructive attitude that she herself had taken in this situation, the truth began to take hold within her that her father really had died when she was only eight years old, that he had been laid away in a grave, and that she would not look upon his face again.

Shortly afterward I had a call from her husband and he said, "What is happening with my wife? For two nights in succession she has cried almost all night long, sobbing till her whole body is shaking. I am very much alarmed. Has something gone wrong in the counseling?"

I explained that nothing had gone wrong, that in fact things were working out better than I dared hope, that the grief of his wife was on behalf of her dead father.

"Let her continue to cry," I said. "Don't try to stop her, because this weeping will end of itself shortly."

That is what happened, and in successive interviews she learned how to transfer to her husband the affection that she had reserved for her dead father.

One month later I had a telephone call from the young doctor. He said, "Our marriage now is filled with a happiness that we have never known before. It is as though we are on our honeymoon. We have a joy and happiness in each other that is beyond measure."

Their Christian faith stood them in good stead, too, and while the doctor's young wife has given up hope of seeing her father in this world, she has a deeper, truer hope that death is not the end or the extinction of life but the entrance upon a larger spiritual existence in the nearer presence of God.

What I have outlined is drawn from the New Testament attitude toward death and grief. When, for instance, Paul begins to list the powers that might threaten to separate us from Christ, he names death first of all but brushes it quickly aside. This was the spirit of all the apostles and evangelists of the early Church. When Stephen was dying, he said, "Lord Jesus, receive my spirit." If we too can enter into a like faith, then solemn, portentous death will be defeated. It will not be necessary for us to preserve the material possessions of loved ones who have gone or to erect around them a sort of shrine at which we engage in what is almost idolatry. After the death of her husband, Pierre, Mme. Curie kept the clothing he wore when he was knocked down and killed in the streets of Paris. From time to time she would bring out these blood-clotted garments and kiss them passionately until one day they were torn from her hands by her sister and burned in the fire.

We know that Christ triumphed over death and our dear ones triumph in him. Wherefore, when death lays its hand on some friend or loved one, we are not plunged into hopeless grief, since faith teaches us that those who have walked with God go on from strength to strength in the life of perfect service of his Heavenly Kingdom.

A fifth cause of widespread tension and inner turmoil in modern life is the anxiety of guilt. At this point it is well to distinguish between neurotic guilt and real guilt. Neurotic guilt has no basis in fact but is due to inner emotional conflicts which must be resolved. Real guilt is guilt resulting from actual moral transgression. Here we are dealing with real guilt. Neurotic guilt lies almost wholly in the province of the psychiatrist. Guilt is the source of the greater part of our anxieties today.

A British scientist, Sir Oliver Lodge, said some years ago that "modern man is not worrying about his sins." Indeed this may still be true, but he is worrying about the strains and tensions that press upon him and the haunting anxieties that torment him. Many of these are the direct results of a sense of guilt— guilt which has been repressed and largely forgotten.

One of the unfailing penalties of sin is guilt. The Bible teaches this truth in all of its sixty-six books. Genesis 3 gives that delightfully poetic description of God walking in the garden in the cool of day. He is looking for Adam. "Adam," he calls, "where are you? Where are you, Adam?" But there is no answer, for Adam is hiding amid the trees. God seeks him out and finds him and our first parent answers, "I was afraid . . . and I hid myself." The inevitable result of disobeying God's commandments is fear. "I was afraid." That statement is as modern as the last automobile off the assembly line. Yet not everyone is alert to the menace lurking under the surface of sin. It looks so appealing, so glamorous, so enticing. It offers us "a good time," and for companionship "gay people."

A young man begins to wonder why he has so long been old-fashioned, governing his life by outmoded moral maxims. But now he's going to change all that. He'll make his own standards. He will decide what is right and what is wrong. He'll scrap the Ten Commandments. He'll be the master of his fate and the captain of his soul. So he plunges in, and ever since he has not known a single day or night free from fear. A knock sounds at his door. A stranger is waiting there. When he opens the door, guilt walks in and makes its home with him.

A few years ago the English poet W. H. Auden went to a Fifty-second Street night club in New York. Seating himself at a table he studied the faces of the men and women gathered there. He saw evidences of futility, boredom, and disillusionment. Turning over the menu on his table, he wrote these words:

Faces along the bar
Cling to their average day:
The lights must never go out,
The music must always play, . . .
Lest we should see where we are,
Lost in a haunted wood,
Children afraid of the night
Who have never been happy or good.[8]

Here in truth is a vivid picture of our modern predicament: a bold brazen front with inner anxieties and fears, sophistication coupled with guilt and self-accusation—symptoms of a sick society.

An American naturalist was walking one day along the Atlantic seashore watching for specimens of primitive forms of life. His attention was suddenly arrested by a strange-looking object at the edge of the water. It appeared to be an immense bird. It was an eagle with a large metal trap fastened to one of its feet. Hundreds of miles away on some mountain slope the huge bird had dropped into the jaws of this trap. The noble creature struggled with all its might and finally flew off with the trap and a bit of chain attached. But it was fatally handicapped in its search for food and at last, worn out with struggle, it fell at the margin of the sea to die of exhaustion, the trap of torture still clinging to its foot.

This story told by a naturalist is a parable of human life. Tens of thousands of people, like that eagle, carry a galling burden everywhere they go. It saps their energy and depletes their resources, until exhausted and defeated they give up the struggle with the torture still clinging to them. What is the burden that so many people carry? It is the anxiety of guilt, ever-present, debilitating, energy-sapping.

Our fears and anxieties browbeat and torment and condemn

[8] From "September 1, 1939" in *The Collected Poetry of W. H. Auden* (New York: Random House, Inc., 1945), reprinted by permission of the publisher.

us. A sensitive imagination, when indulged too much, can produce distressing fears. In many cases only the grace of God can give deliverance. Anyone who has looked deeply into human life is aware of the fact that lengthening shadows of ourselves are cast backward to the past and forward to the future. The past and the future, rather than the present, are the main sources of our anxieties. The past can be a dreadful tyrant. We have all made this discovery. It is constantly bringing up memories that, like the ghost of Banquo in Shakespeare's *Macbeth*, shake their gory locks at us and disturb the happiness of life's feast. Sometimes these memories come in crowds, painful memories and impeachments: foolish things that we have done, bitter words that should have gone unspoken, and the follies of undisciplined years we are now judging in the light of sad experience. Our weaknesses and wickedness alike trail their ugly shadows across memory's screen, and we are disquieted and made anxious.

"If only we had done otherwise!" we say. "If only we had not taken that wrong turning in the road or made that lamentable decision." If our morbid sensibilities be indulged—if we continue this bitter brooding, this mood of melancholy—then self-confidence and self-respect are destroyed, and we become incapacitated. We have been forced by anxiety to take a most futile form of escape.

Dr. Karen Horney has said, "A certain amount of self-confidence is a prerequisite for any achievement." How can we have self-confidence when the past becomes for us a deep and darksome pit, and through the open door of memory demons of fear come trooping out to plague us? More often than not, this disease of the human spirit is beyond man's medicine. Only God's ministering fingers can reach these wounds to heal them.

"God paints in many colors," G. K. Chesterton once wrote, "but he never paints so gorgeously as when he paints in white."

There is the crimson of the sunset, the blue of the ocean, the green of the valley, the scarlet of the poppy, but white is God's best color for human souls burdened with baneful memories of the past. "Though your sins be as scarlet, they shall be as white as snow; though they be red like crimson, they shall be as wool" (Isa. 1:18). These promises of the Word of God fall like sweetest music upon troubled human souls. The remedy for dark fear is faith, and faith has as her companions forgiveness, love, and peace.

Dr. Stopford Brooks, a great preacher of the Church of England in an earlier century, observed that the Ayrshire ministers in Scotland had never truly presented this truth to Robert Burns. They thundered of the law and the judgment, but stopped there, and their condemnation simply threw Burns back on his own resources. "Burns," says Dr. Brooks, "was always coming to himself like the Prodigal Son and saying, 'I will arise and go to my Father,'" but he never got more than half way. Sorry and ashamed, he wanted to start life anew, but his repentance ended before it had well begun. He did not see the Father, as Jesus revealed him, the One who was the friend of every defeated soul and who came to seek and to save the lost.

"It is impossible," says Seneca, "for a man of himself to escape. It must be that someone stretch forth a hand and draw him out." Wherever there is a man or a woman who, sick of repeated defeat and failure, reaches out for help, he will feel an answering touch, a Hand that will lift him up from the miry clay and set his feet on a rock. He will hear a voice saying, "I, even I, am he that blotteth out thy transgressions, and I will not remember thy sins" (Isa. 43:25).

The best news in the world is the news of a God who freely forgives, who takes the follies and the mistakes and sins of the past, and consigns them to the divine oblivion. Then we can face life with new courage, crying triumphantly with the

Psalmist, "In God have I put my trust: I will not be afraid what man can do unto me" (Ps. 56:11).

Even as the past is robbed of its power to hurt, so the future also will hold no terror for us, for the universe is no longer a blank, inscrutable mystery. It becomes the home of a wise and gracious Providence who shapes our destiny and guides us to our journey's end. "In God I have put my trust" is the prescription for anxiety. These words sincerely spoken, deeply believed in, will cure us of cowardice and panic and bring us the healing of calmness and confidence.

There is one remedy and only one for real guilt—the forgiveness of Almighty God. It alone is adequate, for it cleanses, lightens, and transforms a burdened and desperate soul. The supreme fact of the Christian Gospel is that God forgives our sins. The past is blotted out—the past so full of failure and regret—and the future is all our own. Divine forgiveness means reconciliation with God. The barrier that has stood so long between the soul and God is swept away and fellowship with him is restored.

Who among us can live through these exacting and anxious days without feeling an almost desperate need of some divine Power that will fortify his soul? Where may we look for such a mighty ally? The story of the Transfiguration in the Gospels answers that question. In the last painting to come from his inspired brush, Raphael interprets this passage. In "The Transfiguration" we see the mountaintop and Jesus resplendent in the glory of heaven lifted up from the earth with Moses and Elijah, and on the ground the prostrate disciples shielding their eyes from this unwonted splendor. A second scene appears on the lower part of the canvas: the valley beneath and desperate human need. But the genius of Raphael is revealed in this—he makes all the lines down in that valley lead directly to the mountaintop and to the person of Christ. Even an afflicted boy in a paroxysm of frenzy with one uplifted arm points toward the summit of the mountain, indicating the source of all help and healing. This is the artist's message: the answer to problems beyond man's power to solve is to bring the light and healing of heaven to bear upon them.

How graphically the story is told by the Evangelist (Mark 9:14ff.)! The desperate father comes to Jesus and cries, "If you can do anything, have pity on us and help us." Jesus replies, turning the "if" back upon the father, "If *you* can! All things are possible to him who believes." Linking his own undefeatable confidence in God to the wavering and imperfect faith of the distracted father, Jesus makes the lad every whit whole.

Man in his despair still cries, "O God, if you can do anything, help me." And the divine reply invariably comes, "If *you* can. If *you* will." All around us today are anxious, frustrated, despairing, isolated souls. To them, like a rope thrown by strong hands to a struggling man about to be swallowed up in dark waters, comes a voice of hope: "All things are possible to him who believes."

A woman past middle age, who had been a church member for years and one of the most respected persons in her community, asked for help with a problem of increasing nervousness. I soon discovered a history of intermittent migraine headaches and depression. The situation became more and more acute with frequent fainting spells. In one of these, shortly before her visit to me, she had sustained a severe cut on her head.

"Shouldn't you have consulted a medical doctor about these symptoms?" I asked.

"That is exactly what I have done," she replied.

"Well, what did he say about them?"

"He gave me a series of physical tests," she said, "and brought in some laboratory findings. His verdict was, 'So far as this physical examination goes, I can't find a thing wrong with you nor can I find any reason for the symptoms you complain of.

Are you sure that there is nothing on your mind that worries you?' "

There was nothing she could recall.

It developed after several interviews that she was a superbly trained personal secretary and was now retired on pension. She had plenty of time for reflection. A strong recollection came back to her of an episode that had occurred thirty-five years before this time. It concerned her relations with the head of the firm. She was, of course, quite young then and it was easy to see that she must have been a most attractive person. She frankly confessed that an affair had developed between herself and the manager of the large organization for which she worked. This relationship continued for almost six years undetected. The manager was a married man with a family of two small children. Though she had never married, now, more than three decades later, her past had caught up with her. Her mind was full of regrets and powerful feelings of guilt with steadily increasing anxieties. She had been brought up in a home where as a child she was given strict moral instruction. Consequently, she could not forgive herself for what had happened and, as is usually the case in such situations, she resorted to self-punishment. The headaches, the depressions, and the fainting spells were all a part of the mechanism of self-punishment. She was taking it out on herself for the wrong that she had done.

SELF-PUNISHMENT

The fact of self-punishment is met frequently by all counselors wherever there have been severe guilt feelings, and pastoral counselors and psychotherapists are ever on the alert for such manifestations. If people today have lost their sense of sin, how shall we explain the fact that so many of them are constantly punishing themselves for their misdoings?

When this woman had made full confession, she was almost

overcome by emotion. In such situations, as we have already noted, full and complete release for the contrite confessor can be gained only through the divine forgiveness. The result of this emancipating experience was an immediate relaxation of the tension that had gripped her so long. In a moment or two she was smiling through her tears.

I have always made it a practice to ask persons coming through this kind of experience to offer a prayer of thanksgiving to God for the forgiveness that has been received and accepted. This woman offered such a prayer. It was deeply moving in its sincerity and was full of gratitude.

Without exception penitents have to learn that in addition to God's forgiveness, and indeed simultaneously with it, we must forgive ourselves and be willing to accept ourselves as forgiven persons. Secondly, all self-punishment must cease. There is no reason now why we should punish ourselves since we are forgiven by God.

The amount of mental torture that human beings inflict upon themselves, especially through the anxiety of guilt, is almost incredible. It can mar the deepest happiness. It takes the song out of people's hearts and the light from their eyes. It leaves them in shallows of despondency and of misery.

THE PSYCHIATRIC OUT

In cases such as this psychiatrists sometimes seek to apply a "psychiatric out." The patient is told that she was passing through a period of mental confusion or temporary elation when the offense was committed. In any case, the individual is assured that the so-called wrongdoing was due more to sickness than to sin. There are times when such an approach has worked. If people have had a strong moral upbringing, however, seldom are they willing to accept such suggestions. They will be satisfied only when the breach in their relationship with God has been healed. They are oppressed with a sense of separation from God, withdrawal of the divine approval, alienation, hostility. Only the assurance that God has forgiven them will bridge this chasm. When, like the Prodigal Son, "they come to themselves" and return to the Father, the old happy satisfying relationship of Father and child is once again renewed.

A woman seventy-six years of age sought help. Her husband accompanied her. He wished to talk with me, he said, before I saw his wife. He told me that his wife had become very difficult to live with. Most of the time she was in deep depression and full of resentments. She resented the illness that kept her from her social engagements and particularly from the bridge parties she enjoyed. Since her only daughter was married, she had more time on her hands for recreation.

"I hope," said her husband, "that you will be able to do something for her or at least that you can improve this situation. I ask it for her sake and also for my own because life has become almost intolerable in our home."

On the subject of her problem, she admitted that basically she was living in a vicious circle. Five or six years earlier she had attempted suicide but was rescued in time. She felt that she had committed a mortal sin in this suicidal attempt and as she brooded on it a deeper depression resulted. Now, her doctor said, there was fresh danger of another attempt at suicide. A psychotherapist had told her that she was sick in her mind at the time she had made the previous suicidal attempt and that therefore she should not hold it against herself. Her reply was that she knew perfectly well what she was doing and had done it deliberately. It was obvious to me as I talked with her that the previous line of attack on the problem was quite unproductive.

There are situations in which the most constructive method of dealing with a sense of sin is to effect a healing not by lessening the inner conflict but by temporarily heightening it. It is important, of course, that a counselor should know what he is doing at this point because there are certain extreme forms of guilt consciousness which are a factor in serious mental illness.

I made no attempt to weaken the woman's sense of contrition for the attempted suicide and agreed with her that it was wrong and sinful. But I assured her that the situation was not hopeless. In fact, it makes God's promise all the more wonderful, that he stands ready to forgive us our sins, to blot out our offenses, and to assist us in a new beginning.

Dr. Anton T. Boisen[9] cites an instance of a patient who had undergone treatment but still suffered from a feeling of "unspeakable worry." At this time the patient came into the hands of Dwight L. Moody, who brought to him in his penitence the assurance of God's forgiveness. The result was an immediate release of tension. "It was exactly what the patient needed," says Dr. Boisen. "He felt himself directly forgiven by God. Now he had a new role in life. With this new beginning he had something to live for and work for." It was not otherwise with the woman who came to me. She accepted joyfully the divine forgiveness and immediately experienced a new sense of release, of well-being, and of healing. I was in contact with this woman up to the time of her natural death at the age of eighty-one. Not once had this stubborn sense of guilt, with its accompanying depression, returned to her.

In such instances it is rarely necessary to bring to the sufferer's attention the theology of forgiveness. In only one case that I can recall were questions asked on this point. Indeed it is inadvisable for the counselor to launch into theological explanations of the basis of forgiveness. People who have had even a slight Christian training seem to have thoroughly imbibed the teaching that in the cross of Christ, God has extended his forgiveness

[9] *Religion in Crisis and Custom* (New York: Harper & Brothers, 1955), p. 52.

to man, on the one hand expressing his judgment on sin and on the other hand revealing the lengths to which divine love will go to bestow forgiveness. If during an interview one gets too much involved in theology, the patient may employ the discussion of that theme to start an argument or to find a means of escape from facing his own dilemma.

Both the Old and New Testaments contain wonderful promises of the divine absolution. One of these is: "I, even I, am he that blotteth out thy transgressions . . . and will not remember thy sins" (Isa. 43:25). Sometimes one meets with contrite persons who find it difficult to believe that God can forgive our sins and may ask, "How are they to be blotted out?" It may be helpful to employ a very simple mode of teaching—to write lightly with pencil the word "sins" on a piece of paper and then rub the word out with an eraser. Ask the penitent, "What was on that paper a moment ago?" He replies, "The word 'sins.' "

Then ask him, "Where is the word now?"

He says, "It is gone."

You ask, "Gone where?"

"Well, it is just erased. It doesn't exist any longer."

Then says the counselor, "That is exactly what God says, 'I, even I, am he that blotteth out thy transgressions.' In this promise God adds, 'and I will not remember thy sins.' In other words, they are dropped into the divine oblivion."

If a counselee, overwhelmed by the magnitude of his offenses, has difficulty in believing that God will forgive his sins, the spiritual counselor must endeavor to mediate that forgiveness. He will say to the penitent individual, "As you have told me of your wrongdoing, your mistakes, your failures, have you sensed any spirit of judgmentalism on my part? Have I censured or condemned you for the wrong you have done?" (These questions may be safely asked if the counselor has achieved rapport with the counselee. It is doubtful that he would have

reached this point in the interview if a working relationship
had not already been established.)

The counselee's reply will be something like this, "No, I haven't
detected any such reaction on your part. I think you have been
truly understanding." To which the counselor will reply,
"Whatever understanding and compassion I have manifested
I have learned from the Great Physician, Jesus Christ. You recall
how tenderly he dealt with the woman taken in adultery who
was dragged into his presence in the temple by a group of
religious leaders. The Master's verdict was, 'Let him that is
without sin cast the first stone at her,' and to the woman he
said, 'Neither do I condemn thee. Go and sin no more.' As you
recall these words of Jesus, remember that he also said, 'He that
hath seen me hath seen the Father.' He has revealed to us the
character of the unseen God. Remember it is this God who
promises complete and unlimited forgiveness to all who in
penitence and contrition seek it." (John 8:3-11, 14:9.)

After the divine forgiveness has been received and accepted,
a prayer of thanksgiving, already referred to, should be offered
by the penitent counselee. Then write out for such persons the
first four verses of the 103rd Psalm:

> Bless the Lord, O my soul: and all that is
> within me, bless his holy name.
> Bless the Lord, O my soul, and forget not all
> his benefits:
> Who forgiveth all thine iniquities; who healeth
> all thy diseases;
> Who redeemeth thy life from destruction; who
> crowneth thee with loving-kindness and tender
> mercies.

Everything the penitent individual needs at this point will
be found in these verses. They should be memorized and repeated frequently through the day and in the last moments before

sleep at night. This spiritual message will establish and strongly confirm the experience through which the counselee has come. The willingness to make amends or to offer restitution for wrongs done to others is an integral part of the experience of contrition and forgiveness. Great care must be taken, however, lest the attempt at restitution do more harm than good to the penitent and to other persons as well.

The Bible contains many such helpful verses which may be usefully given to people who have come for counseling because of a sense of guilt. I find that the verses are doubly appreciated if they are written in longhand by the counselor. This adds a personal touch that is helpful. Appended herewith are a group of such verses applicable to this kind of situation. It will be seen how far-reaching are the assurances the Bible gives of forgiveness. We are told that not only does God blot out our transgressions but that he will cease to remember them. He will put them from us as far as the east is from the west; that is, he will remove them an infinite distance. He will cast our sins behind his back; that is, he will come between us and our sins.

Thou art a God ready to pardon, gracious and merciful. [Neh. 9:17]

Thou hast forgiven the iniquity of thy people, thou hast covered all their sin. [Ps. 85:2]

Thou, Lord, art good, and ready to forgive; and plenteous in mercy unto all them that call upon thee. [Ps. 86:5]

Who forgiveth all thine iniquities; who healeth all thy diseases. [Ps. 103:3]

Thou hast cast all my sins behind thy back. [Isa. 38:17]

I, even I, am he that blotteth out thy transgressions for mine own sake, and will not remember thy sins. [Isa. 43:25]

I have blotted out, as a thick cloud, thy transgressions, and, as a cloud, thy sins. [Isa. 44:22]

I will forgive their iniquity, and I will remember their sin no more. [Jer. 31:34]

I will pardon all their iniquities. [Jer. 33:8]

The Lord will not cast off for ever. [Lam. 3:31]

To the Lord our God belong mercies and forgivenesses. [Dan. 9:9]

Who is a God like unto thee, that pardoneth iniquity, and passeth by the transgression of this remnant of his heritage? He retaineth not his anger for ever, because he delighteth in mercy. [Mic. 7:18]

Neither do I condemn thee: go, and sin no more. [John 8:11]

Blessed are they whose iniquities are forgiven, and whose sins are covered. [Rom. 4:7]

Forgetting those things which are behind, and reaching forth unto those things which are before, I press toward the mark for the prize of the high calling of God in Christ Jesus. [Phil. 3:13, 14]

Now once in the end of the world hath he appeared to put away sin by the sacrifice of himself. [Heb. 9:26]

If we confess our sins, he is faithful and just to forgive us our sins, and to cleanse us from all unrighteousness. [I John 1:9]

I make all things new. [Rev. 21:5]

It should be evident from these Scripture passages that the Bible is the most heartening, bracing, optimistic book in the world. It never despairs of man. It offers him boundless hope. It promises to the contrite reconciliation, inner renewal, and moral recovery. It tells of open doors, of forgiven pasts, of renewed opportunities, and of the white highway of God's will. It points the way to victory over the soul-destroying anxiety of guilt.

In this chapter we have dealt with five types of anxiety: economic anxiety, the anxiety of worry, fear of an atomic or hydrogen holocaust, the anxiety of grief, and the anxiety of guilt. These by no means exhaust the anxieties that trouble mankind today but they include the most destructive of them.

A sound philosophy of life is a fundamental necessity in any attempt to master our anxieties. The chief ingredient in such a philosophy should be faith—faith in God, faith in ourselves, faith in the dignity and worth of every human creature as a child of God, faith in man's ability to work out his problems in the spirit of co-operation and good will, faith in the moral and spiritual values that undergird his life. When we are garrisoned by such a philosophy, no opportunity is afforded to anxieties to become entrenched in our lives. They lose their power over us.

We should remember that practically all our inappropriate fears and anxieties have been learned. By the same token, we can unlearn and banish them. We should, therefore, drag them out from the dark corners of the mind into the clear light of reason, examining them critically and seeking to determine their origin.

Dr. Karen Horney has pointed out in one of her helpful books[10] that self-analysis may be a potent factor in the achievement of healthy-mindedness. This is especially true if we possess a robust faith and a sound philosophy of life. Then we shall possess resources upon which to draw. Great convictions and positive beliefs furnish the motive power for achieving a disciplined, courageous personality.

One of the finest examples in history of such a person is General Gordon—Gordon of Khartoum, as he was frequently called. He was universally respected and beloved. In battle he was almost invincible and was renowned for his utter fearlessness. In China he led his troops into action armed only with a cane. Joined with his prowess as a military commander was a great capacity for human compassion. In a *New York Times* book review of the latest life of General Gordon[11] the reviewer writes, "The extraordinary courage to which he owed much of his power was derived from faith: he was in God's hands, all the events were God's will, and he was in no more danger when exposing himself under fire than when reading a newspaper in his club."

It is impossible to conceive of a man like General Gordon becoming prey to unreasoning fears or destructive anxieties. His

[10] *Self-Analysis* (New York: W. W. Norton & Co., Inc., 1942).
[11] *Gordon of Khartoum* by Lord Elton (New York: Alfred A. Knopf, 1955).

faith provided an inviolable armor. In the light of such a victorious personality we can better understand why psychiatrists are saying today that the sovereign remedy for every kind of fear is faith.

The prophet Ezekiel furnishes us with a striking picture of the true posture of faith. He had seen a vision of God lifted up in glory and majesty and prostrated himself before him. At that moment he heard the Voice divine saying, "Son of man, stand upon thy feet, and I will speak unto thee" (2:1). Here is the highest ideal of healthy-mindedness and self-mastery—a man not seeking to escape from life but God-conscious, self-reliant, emancipated from fear, standing erect before his Maker awaiting the divine will.

3 Drowning Troubles
in Drink

One day as I was returning to my church from pastoral calls in a hospital, I had a strong intuitive feeling that I should visit a young woman with whom I recently had had several interviews. As urgent work was awaiting me in my study, I pushed the thought from my mind, but it kept returning so powerfully that I gave the address of the girl's home to the taxi driver. Over a quarter of a century's experience in pastoral work had taught me that such impulses should not be disregarded. As many pastors have learned, one must remain spiritually sensitive to these promptings.

A month or two earlier I had visited Jean's home at the suggestion of her mother. The mother had telephond me without her daughter's knowledge because she had become alarmed at some suicidal hints expressed by Jean. I found her drinking steadily. She had been on a binge and was tapering off on beer. I offered no condemnation of her drinking nor did I tell her she should make a more valiant attempt to quit it. (Later I heard her tell a group of seminary students that she never would have accepted help from me had I shown revulsion to her drinking on this occasion.) In the interviews that followed that first visit to her home, she refused to admit that her drinking was out of control.

"I can handle this thing myself," she said. "When I really make up my mind that I want to quit, I'll quit."

I asked her if she had ever attended an Alcoholics Anonymous meeting.

"Yes, I have," she replied. "I thought I would see what was going on there, but I don't belong with that crowd. It's all right for them. They can't handle their drinking. With me it's different. I can." It was easy to see that she had built up a defense of arrogance and pride against all attempts by anyone to help her. I knew perfectly well that nothing could be done until she was ready to accept help and that that time had not yet come.

These reflections passed through my mind as I approached her mother's home. In response to my ring at the door of a tenth-floor apartment, Jean's mother appeared. Her face was as white as death.

"Oh," she said, "thank God you got my message. I have been trying all over the city to reach you. I called the church, the hospital you visited, and other places. Well, anyway, you got it. I hope you're not too late."

"What message did you send?" I asked her.

"You didn't get it? Well, never mind, you're here now. Jean's done it this time."

"Done what?" I asked.

"Killed herself," answered the mother.

"Is she dead?" I inquired.

"Not quite, but pretty nearly."

"Did you call the doctor?" I asked.

"Yes," she replied, "but he was on his way to another emergency call and had time only to give her a 'hypo.' He said he would be back just as quickly as he could. Come in."

She led me to a bedroom where her daughter lay looking far more dead than alive. On this as on other occasions my two and a half years' training as a nurse stood me in good stead. I tried to find her pulse at the wrist and at the temple but couldn't feel even a flicker. Her hands and arms were cold. Her fingernails were blue. Her hands were closing and when one pulled the fingers open, they snapped back again to a half-closed position, indicating the approach of rigor mortis. In the corner of the room were empty whisky bottles and on the table a phial that had contained barbiturates.

Knowing how important it was to arouse her, I took off my coat and with the help of her mother began to massage her arms and shoulders, to lift her up and throw her back on the pillow, to push her from one to the other of us on the bed as violently as possible. When she began to show some slight evidence of consciousness, I asked her mother to brew a strong cup of coffee. I continued the attempts to arouse Jean from her almost complete stupor until the mother brought the coffee. When it was sufficiently cool, I gave her a few drops on a spoon and waited and listened for results. One must make certain that the liquid is going to the stomach and not to the lungs. In the latter case the patient's sputtering and coughing will reveal a paralysis of the esophagus muscles. However, she was able to swallow it all. Talking to her and shaking her at intervals, I succeeded in getting her to drink the entire cupful. At the end of ten minutes there was a faint flicker in her pulse. We gave her more coffee and continued the massaging. At the end of half an hour the patient was able to talk a little, though incoherently, but she did not recognize even her own mother. By this time the doctor returned and took over. He said the hypodermic injection he had administered, coupled with the massage and caffeine, had given her a real fighting chance. For three days and three nights she was under the constant care of nurses and by the aid of skillful medical attention recovered completely.

Two weeks later she was in the consulting room of our church looking much the worse for wear. All her defiance and pride were now gone.

"I am ready to admit," she said, "that alcohol has got me down. I guess I am an alcoholic after all. Now what do you want me to do?"

I recognized in Jean's words that the moment of surrender was approaching—the moment of genuine hope for her.

"Jean," I said, "you've had a couple of weeks in which to think over this experience. What insights have you gained? What lessons have you learned?"

"Well," she replied, "I feel pretty silly about the things I said concerning the A.A. people. I had thought of them as weak sisters and felt that I was stronger than the whole lot of them. I boasted I had will power to win my way through anything, and that if I ever reached the point where they were—to stand up in a meeting and say, 'I am an alcoholic'—I would just feel that I was groveling in the dust and would be ashamed to hold up my head. I have learned how utterly stupid that reasoning is. I now know that my will power is not worth the snap of a finger and that my pride was just a device to save face for myself. I suppose you recognized my suicide attempt. I couldn't see any way out and figured that the best thing to do was to end it all. Then as I lay on that bed day after day convalescing, a new line of thought came to me. It suddenly dawned on me that I had been trying desperately to run away from life and I saw that my alcoholism was actually slow suicide. Well, now I'm ready to come to terms with life and with God. I am sick of running away and for the first time in my experience I realize that it's got to be absolute, unconditional surrender. I'm honestly ready now to accept your help and the help of God. The fight is out of me. I am ready to be led. You could hardly believe how much inner peace has come to me since I reached this point in my own thinking."

Instantly there came to my mind a conversation I had had some years before with Bill, one of the co-founders of A.A. I asked him then, "What will Alcoholics Anonymous say to a man who doesn't want help, who says that he can go it on his own, that his own will power will carry him through?"

"Well," said Bill, "we say, 'All right, you will have to go it on your own. We can't force you to accept what we have to offer. You have to come to us willing to accept it. You must surrender—surrender to life, surrender to the help we are able to give you, surrender to God.' "

"What happens then, Bill?" I asked him.

He replied, "We have to wait until John Barleycorn kindles a still hotter fire under him. His defiance and his pride will not give in until something akin to a disaster has overtaken him. Then many of them come back and say, 'All right, I'm ready now.' "

It had taken the near approach of death to bring Jean to her senses. I read her the first three steps of Alcoholics Anonymous:

Step One

"We admitted we were powerless over alcohol—that our lives had become unmanageable."

Step Two

"Came to believe that a Power greater than ourselves could restore us to sanity."

Step Three

"Made a decision to turn our will and our lives over to the care of God as we understood him."

Here are the three essential elements in these "steps":

1. The admission of defeat—that life has become unmanageable.

2. What we cannot do of ourselves can be done with the help of God.

3. We resolve to turn our lives over to the care of God. We make a complete surrender.

Jean reacted as follows: "I can see now that there must be a change in the rulership of my life. I have been playing God up to this point and I must surrender that control. I have been afraid of life. I've been so afraid of life that I was willing to take death instead of trying to live. Now that I am making this surrender, I want it to be complete, as you suggest—a surrender to life, a surrender to reality, and a surrender to God. I'm not going to fight any more. From this moment, with God's help, the desire to be sober is going to be stronger than anything else in my life."

Under the direction of her physician, Jean had already undergone a "drying-out" process in a hospital. I knew that she would require continuous help and guidance from understanding people, so I contacted some A.A. members in my own church. Every alcoholic who is mastering his problem should be in touch with A.A. because these people know exactly what they are talking about for they have been through the fire. They know all the rationalizations, all the excuses, all the comforting words of self-pity. That is, they talk the language of an alcoholic and have the right answer on the tip of their tongues. Moreover, they are able to introduce a new A.A. member to other alcoholics who need help, and every time he stretches out a helping hand to somebody who is floundering in the morass of alcoholism, he takes out some additional insurance for himself against any possible personal relapse. Everyone needs the comradeship of people who are trying to live at their best, but to the alcoholic it is indispensable. He is taking a terrible risk if he thinks he can do it alone. Jean now found that Alcoholics Anonymous was something quite different from what she had thought and that many of its members are highly intelligent, respectable, socially acceptable people.

I asked her to join a group in our church that is devoted to helping people. As I have previously indicated, the members of this group encourage one another at their weekly meetings by telling of Biblical verses they have found to steady and sustain them. It was an interesting and impressive experience to listen to Jean's verses. It had been eighteen years since she had had any active contact with a Christian church, but she brought to her reading of the Bible a deep sense of reality and remarkable spiritual insight. Life had taught her lessons the hard way and there was always a sense of reality and deep understanding of life in her comments on Scripture passages.

In my own congregation I have half a dozen members of Alcoholics Anonymous. They are my right-hand helpers. At any hour of the day or night they are ready to come when help is needed. Physicians, pastors, teachers, and all others concerned with the welfare of people should remember in a case of serious difficulty with an alcoholic to enlist the help of one or two members of A.A.

THE TWELVE STEPS

One of the prime modes of therapy for alcoholism is found in the moral and spiritual insights of the Twelve Steps of Alcoholics Anonymous, which appear at the end of this chapter. A process of re-education must be undertaken and if it is not possible to contact an A.A. group, the counselor or pastor who is dealing with the alcoholic must try to apply the insights of these Twelve Steps.

Each time a member of A.A. states "I am an alcoholic," he

is renewing in his thinking and feeling that moment of surrender that is so all-important. The new life upon which he has entered can be developed and expressed by a new interest in things outside himself and in persons, beginning with his own family. It has been well said that the alcoholic cannot keep the precious gift of sobriety unless he continues to give it away, that is, unless he is helping other alcoholics to stand on their feet and face life serenely and courageously. All Twelve Steps in A.A.'s helpful program are important but the first three are absolutely essential.

Everyone who has to deal with an alcoholic should know that denunciation and censoriousness are absolutely useless in talking with a victim of drink. There is no word of contempt that he has not already called himself. What he needs is not condemnation but personal insight and hope. An alcoholic will sometimes refuse for months or even years to admit that he is already defeated. During that period entreaty, tears, threats, and censure all fail.

This refusal is aptly illustrated by a businessman, a little under forty years of age, whose condition first came to my attention through an interview with his wife. She had come in to say that she was gravely troubled about him. At night on his way home from work he would stop at a bar for several drinks. He had been keeping liquor in the closet of his bedroom and taking a drink or two after he came home. First he did this openly, then furtively, and when his wife said that she didn't want liquor in the home at all, he began to hide it in various places. She had talked the situation over with her husband, pointing out to him that their two children were now becoming involved. The older child was a boy of twelve. He had a sister aged seven. She said the children were beginning to notice at the dinner table that something was the matter with their dad.

A few days later her husband came in and talked with me

about their son who would shortly be going to preparatory school. When we had disposed of the prep school matter, I asked him, "How are things going with you personally?"

He answered jauntily that business was never better and that he thought he was making progress with the firm.

I asked him again how things were going with his personal life. "Fine," he said. "I've got everything in hand nicely."

As he said this he looked at me suspiciously and asked, "Have you gotten the impression from anyone that things haven't been going well with me?"

I replied that I did not depend on impressions from anyone except the person concerned. I wanted his word on the subject.

He said, "Well, perhaps one of the boys at the office may have suggested that I have been drinking. I know one of my friends in the firm seemed to be a little anxious about this, but there is no good reason for his concern. Everything is okay. Don't you worry. I haven't met anything yet in life that I couldn't handle."

The next time his wife came in it was easy to see that matters had progressively worsened during the previous four months. Her husband had become interested in horse racing and was gambling on the horses. He had lost a lot of money. If things continued the way they had started, he would lose everything including the house they were living in. This time she gave me permission to mention that she had come to see me and had expressed anxiety about his gambling.

I visited them both one night. After the children had gone to bed she brought up the subject of her husband's drinking. I could see that he was quite annoyed. His pride was hurt. I talked quite frankly with him on the subject and he admitted that the only time he gambled was when he had had a drink or two. He was going to quit the liquor and then automatically the gambling would stop.

"I don't know why it is," he said, "but when I'm dead sober, I have no desire whatsoever to gamble. It's only when I'm drinking."

I explained to him that I had no wish to intrude in his life but I had such a deep personal concern and affection for him, for his wife, and for his lovely children that I felt the church and I had a big stake in what was going on. However, he continued to resist help.

During the next six months things grew so serious that the president of the firm warned him to straighten himself out or be replaced. This threw him into a tailspin and he went on a prolonged "binge." One night while under the influence of liquor he went back to the office. When the office staff arrived at a few minutes to nine the next morning, he was "out cold" and lying half dressed on a couch in the outer office. The president of the firm called me to say that they were going to discharge him. I pleaded his case and urged that he be given one more chance. The president agreed, but only on one condition —that the man would personally give the firm some assurance, more tangible and convincing than anything he had promised in the past, that he was straightening himself out. Matters now reached a climax. Faced with this grim situation, he saw that he had to choose between sobriety or ruin. He was no longer on the defensive. This time he produced no alibis or excuses.

"This thing has me licked and I know it," he admitted.

He too came to the point of complete surrender. This did not mean that the struggle was over. In some respects it had only begun. But at last he acknowledged that he was a defeated person. He also became willing to accept the help of God and man. He accepted the two necessary requirements for recovery from uncontrolled alcoholism:

1. He desperately wanted to recover.
2. He believed that he could recover.

One of the hardest battles he had to fight was to acknowledge within himself that he could never again drink any form of alcoholic liquor. Even moderate drinking for him was completely taboo. He had to learn to picture life without the crutch of alcohol. In a series of interviews he co-operated heartily with me as we sought to discover the weakness in his personality that fostered his compulsive drinking. One important fact stands out invariably in the experience of every alcoholic.

An alcoholic is a person who is emotionally immature and therefore cannot face life's difficulties without the temporary and deceptive reinforcement of alcohol.

No one will ever understand the problem of alcoholism who does not grasp the principle just outlined. It is not without good reason that Alcoholics Anonymous have set forth in their Twelve Steps such techniques for moral and spiritual growth as belief in God, making a moral inventory of ourselves, acknowledging and confessing our shortcomings, making amends to those we have injured, helping others who are in difficulties, and by meditation and prayer seeking to make our lives channels of God's power and grace.

Many an alcoholic has confided to me that he could never have made the grade had he not learned to live one day at a time. He couldn't have tolerated the thought of battling his desires and weaknesses and remain sober for a week or a month, but he could manage it for twenty-four hours.

It was the spiritual factor in A.A. that enabled the alcoholic gambler, whose case history I have described, to win through. Three Bible verses became a part of his life.

"I can do all things through Christ who strengthens me."

"If God be for me, who can be against me?"

"The Lord is on my side. I will not fear what man can do unto me."

Day and night he repeated these words thoughtfully and

believingly until his mind was saturated with them. They were meat and drink to him and largely explain how he achieved so thoroughgoing a victory.

Defeat and Surrender

I have often felt that the admission of defeat is the most important step of all. It seems to be the indispensable first step because it is accompanied almost invariably by surrender. Out of this double step of admission of defeat and surrender comes the acceptance of life and increasing self-knowledge. Surrender must not be confused with mere submission. One may submit to the dictates of one's boss, or of one's doctor, or of one's minister, or of one's wife and family, but almost always that type of reaction carries with it a powerful resentment defeating constructive hopes. It must be surrender, full and complete, before the victim has set his feet on the pathway leading to self-mastery; not until he has accepted the mastery of a Higher Power can he achieve self-mastery.

On one occasion some time since, I dined with Dr. Harry M. Tiebout, psychiatrist of Greenwich, Connecticut, who has taken an active part in the Yale University Alcohol Studies. In the course of the dinner he asked, "What do you consider to be the greatest spiritual discovery which you have made in the last five to ten years?"

I answered that the experience of surrender had grown in importance for me, that I felt it was the key to genuine progress in the Christian life. He smiled at this point, and I asked him if he thought there was something amusing about this finding.

"No," he replied, "quite the reverse. Isn't this a coincidence?" He pulled a manuscript out of his pocket and continued, "Here's a copy of an address I gave to a psychiatric society a short time ago."

I looked at the title of the address. It was: "The Importance of Surrender." From it I quote these words: "We can now be more precise in our definition of an act of surrender. It is to be viewed as a moment when the unconscious forces of defiance and grandiosity actually cease effectively to function. When that happens the individual is wide open to reality. He can listen and learn without fighting back. He is receptive to life, not antagonistic. He senses a feeling of relatedness and at-oneness which becomes the source of an inner peace and serenity, the possession of which frees the individual from his compulsion to drink. In other words, an act of surrender is an occasion wherein the individual no longer fights life but accepts it."

This experience is more far-reaching when it goes beyond surrender to life and becomes surrender to God and his will. It is the crucial point with all alcoholics and oftentimes with other persons as well. In stressing surrender in the first three steps of Alcoholics Anonymous the founders of that organization have laid their hands upon what is at the heart of the Christian gospel—the admission of moral and spiritual defeat, the belief that God can give us the victory over our failure, and the resolution to turn our lives over to God. These three steps have been the basis of some of the greatest conversions recorded in religious history. When an alcoholic faces his problem, there is a tremendous struggle. Pride is the great obstacle to be overcome. The alcoholic will say, "I don't belong with that crowd of people in the A.A. meetings. They're just not my class. They're weak people who need the help of something outside themselves, but with me it's different. I can get on top of this problem without any real trouble. All I have to do is make up my mind to do it."

It is hard for anybody to say, "I have failed. I am defeated. Life has got me completely down. I am a slave to alcohol." What a great many people find difficult to understand about the alcoholic is that his will is no longer operative when he is tempted to drink. He is drinking compulsively. That is, his feelings and desires have taken over and are running his life in defiance of any expression of will power. The one point at which the alcoholic will turn from drunkenness to sobriety will be when he wants sobriety so much that he will sacrifice his pride, his sense of prestige, his resistance to surrender, and be willing to say, "I am beaten." Or a woman will say, "I am defeated."

Sometimes this struggle will go on for months, sometimes for years. John Barleycorn may be painfully slow in kindling the fire and often disaster will overtake the individual before he has sought the better way.

At the present time, I am seeing a young woman who has not yet been able to make the surrender. She came to me a year ago when she was nineteen years of age and had just finished her sophomore year at college. Twice she had been before the president on the charge of being found in an intoxicated condition. She had an excellent scholastic record and is a beautiful-looking person. This is her story: "At the age of fourteen when I was alone one time in our home, I came upon beer in the refrigerator and drank some of it. I did this from time to time and got to like it. Quite unknown to my parents I have kept up this practice. So far I have gotten by. I wouldn't have come to you at all on this matter if it weren't that I am getting into an awful mess. I am confused about everything. My moral standards have been sagging badly. I want you to know that this is not the way I'd like to live. I am at my worst if I have been drinking beer for awhile. Strangely enough, I don't care for hard liquor at all and have hardly tasted cocktails. It is always beer. If I have had a few beers, when I go out on a date almost anything goes with me and I have had some pretty scary experiences. I can't seem to think straight after I have been drinking. It seems impossible to know what is right and what is wrong. I wonder if there are any suggestions you could make that would help me."

I explained to her how her moral problem was bound up with her drinking. After further questioning of the young student I discovered that she had never been able to abstain from beer for more than two or three weeks. At the end of that time she would be jittery, feeling terribly self-conscious and tormented with fears. A few drinks would put her right again. "Now," she said, "abstinence for a week is about all I can take." Then a feeling of restlessness and uneasiness comes over her so that she has to drink to feel a sense of stability and self-assurance.

As there were some perplexing features in this case I consulted a psychiatrist who is a specialist on alcohol. After I had described the symptoms, he said without a moment's hesitation, "She's hooked. It's got her solid. She's an alcoholic." When I asked the psychiatrist what her chances were for recovery, he said, "Not too good at present. Because she is so young and healthy, she can take a lot of punishment without being aware of the fact that she is going downhill fast."

When I saw the young woman in later interviews, she scoffed at the idea that she might be an alcoholic. "I can handle this thing. It can't get me down. If I could only settle the moral end of it, I wouldn't have a worry in the world," she said.

Her situation is not yet resolved. I feel quite confident that someday she will make a surrender to reality and to God and discover how poor and shoddy her life has been through these years, but we shall have to wait for that time. Tragically enough she may have to be involved in some kind of disaster before her eyes will be opened, and she will then realize that she has been a prisoner behind walls that her own hands have built and behind bars that her own fingers have fashioned.

WHAT ARE THE DANGER SIGNS THAT ONE IS BECOMING AN ALCOHOLIC?

1. *Are you a morning drinker?* The man or woman who cannot face the problems of the day without the support of alcohol often drinks before 10:00 A.M. Other drinkers who do not suffer from the emotional instability of the alcoholic avoid like the plague that morning drink. The man who needs an "eye opener" in order to overcome the miseries of "the morning after" is one who is already manifesting a dangerous lack of self-control. While his associates are facing the problems of the office, the bank, the store, or the school, he has gone to some bar for "a quick one" or he is tippling in his own home. A few drinks serve as medicine for frayed nerves.

2. *Do you have to bolster yourself with a drink or two if you are going to face a difficult business deal?* If you wish to carry through successfully an interview with the boss or the president of the firm, do you reinforce yourself with alcohol? Do you have a desire to imbibe alcohol the moment difficulty emerges in your home with your wife or other members of the family, or when you are slated to preside at a meeting or to give an address, or to face an unusually heavy responsibility?

3. *From time to time do you have deep feelings of inferiority or an indefinable restlessness and growing tension that is relieved only by alcohol?*

4. *Do you suffer a lot from boredom? Is alcohol your remedy for it?* Boredom may be defined as an excessive awareness of the passing of time. Time becomes an oppressive weight. It moves with leaden feet. So it is necessary to kill time.

5. *Has abstinence become for you a great difficulty or an impossibility?* Have you lost control of yourself and your situation so that you are no longer able to give up alcohol even though you sincerely desire to do so and make solemn resolutions that

you will not touch it again? You may rationalize, excuse yourself, twist and turn, but the one question is: Can you give up alcohol or can't you?

6. *Has your drinking begun to create difficulty and unhappiness in your marriage relationship?* Authorities on this subject have often said that happily married people do not drink to excess. The very fact that one seeks escape or oblivion in alcohol is itself evidence that the marriage is already headed for the rocks.

7. *Do you lack control of your drinking in cases where it will injure your prospects?* If you have an engagement of great importance and even one drink would make a bad impression, will you take that drink from a sense of need?

8. *Instead of drinking for enjoyment and stopping when you wish to, do you drink on with little or no control and in response to a strange inner compulsion?*

9. *Do you protest too much that you are a controlled drinker?* Every alcoholic remembers that he boasted control long after he had lost it. Can you face the truth about yourself and escape years of boundless misery?

10. *Do you find that alcohol is for you becoming a substitute for food? Do you skip meals to consume more alcohol?*

11. *Are you inclined to be a solitary drinker?* Do you hide liquor about the house so that you can sneak an occasional drink?

12. *Do you say repeatedly: "I'll have just one more" when you know you have had several too many?*

13. *Do you go on a "bender" several times a year and also take occasional days off to get rid of a "cold" which is in reality a "hang-over"?*

14. *Are you unwilling to sit down with a trained counselor and discuss the inferiorities, the inordinate pride, and the resentments of your inner life? Do you seek to evade these by means of daydreaming and the use of alcohol?*

If you are compelled to answer "yes" to any three of these fourteen points, you may well be started along the road that leads to the morass of alcoholism.

IMPORTANT FACTS ON ALCOHOLISM

1. There are approximately 4,000,000 alcoholics in the United States.

2. Of these persons 950,000 are suffering from severe chronic alcoholism.

3. The United States Department of Health calls alcoholism the fourth most prevalent disease in the nation. The three more common diseases are cardiac disorders, cancer, and mental illness.

4. In addition to the known alcoholics, there is an indeterminate number, likely several million persons, who are either actual alcoholics but have never reported anywhere for treatment or others who may drink to the extent that they become involved in difficulties but who do not yet manifest the chronic and progressive characteristics of pathological drinking.

5. The chairman of the American Medical Association's Committee on Alcoholism says that his observations in private practice and hospital work lead him to believe that as many as one out of three alcoholics is a woman. Alcoholics Anonymous reports more and more female members.

6. The Subcommittee on Alcoholism of the World Health Organization defines alcoholics as "those excessive drinkers whose dependence upon alcohol has attained such a degree that it shows a noticeable mental disturbance, or an interference with their bodily and mental health, their interpersonal relations, and their smooth social and economic functioning; or who show the prodromal signs of such developments."

7. Most recent estimates by institutes having to do with alcoholic studies suggest that approximately 60,000,000 adults in the United States are users of alcoholic beverages. Only about

7 per cent of these are known alcoholics. However, the 60,000,-000 drinkers constitute the "exposed population" in the matter of alcoholism, for naturally this illness does not exist outside their ranks.

8. One of the most successful agencies in dealing with alcoholism is Alcoholics Anonymous, which is not limited to its estimated 150,000 members. It has demonstrated that with skill and understanding and a spiritual philosophy alcoholics may be reclaimed as useful, productive, respectable, and reasonably well-integrated members of the community.

9. It must be kept clearly in mind that the majority of people partake of alcohol for the sake of the emotional lift they receive. The alcoholic finds that the gap between his way of life and that of the rest of society is less pronounced when he is drinking. Alcohol gives him a feeling of well-being, supports his ego, enables him to overlook his material and financial failures and to forget his loneliness. The very thought of the withdrawal of alcohol frightens him and fills him with insecurity and anxiety.

10. There are six qualities of character to be found in the alcoholic, says Professor David A. Stewart. These are: childishness, sensitiveness, grandiose ideas, impulsiveness, intolerance, and wishful thinking. These qualities become more dominant the more the alcoholic drinks. He reverts to childish ways and dreams.

What Must the Alcoholic Learn During His Recovery?[1]

1. BE CONVINCED from his own experience that his reaction to alcohol is so abnormal that any indulgence for him constitutes a totally undesirable and impossible way of life.

2. RECOGNIZE that the problem of drinking, for him, is not merely a problem of dissipation, but of a dangerous psychopathological reaction to a (for him) pernicious drug.

[1] A Summary of a brochure by Robert V. Seliger, M.D., Chief Psychiatrist, Neuropsychiatric Institute, Baltimore, Maryland, published by The National Committee on Alcohol Hygiene, Inc.

3. CLEARLY UNDERSTAND that, once a man has passed from normal to abnormal drinking, he can *never* learn to control drinking again.

4. COME TO UNDERSTAND that he has been trying to substitute alcoholic fantasy for real achievement in life, and that his effort has been hopeless and absurd.

5. COME TO UNDERSTAND that the motive behind his drinking has been some form of self-expression, some desire to gratify an immature craving for attention, or to escape from unpleasant reality in order to get rid of disagreeable states of mind.

6. REALIZE that any reasonably intelligent and sincere person who is willing to make a sustained effort for a sufficient period of time is capable of learning to live without alcohol.

7. LEARN to be tolerant of other people's mistakes, poor judgment, and bad manners without becoming emotionally disturbed.

8. RECOGNIZE alcoholic daydreaming—about past "good times," favorite bars, etc.—as a dangerous pastime to be inhibited by thinking about his reasons for *not* drinking.

9. LEARN TO WITHSTAND success as well as failure, since pleasant emotions, as well as unpleasant ones, can serve as a "good" excuse for taking a drink.

10. TRY TO ACQUIRE a mature sense of values and learn to be controlled by his judgment instead of by his emotions.

11. LEARN the importance of eating—since the best preventive for that tired nervous feeling which leads to taking a drink is food—and to carry chocolate bars or other candy with him, at all times, to eat between meals and whenever he gets restless, jittery, or tired.

12. LEARN HOW to relax naturally, both mentally and physi-cally, without the use of the narcotic action of alcohol.

13. CAREFULLY FOLLOW a daily self-imposed schedule which, conscientiously carried out, aids in organizing a disciplined personality, developing new habits for old and bringing out a new rhythm of living.

14. NOT BE DISCOURAGED by a feeling of discontent during the early stages of sobriety, but turn this feeling into incentive to action which will legitimately satisfy his desire for self-expression.

15. UNDERSTAND that, besides abstinence, his real goal is a contented and efficient life.

16. APPRECIATE the seriousness of his re-education and regard it as the most important thing in his life.

17. REALIZE that most people seeking psychological help for abnormal drinking are above average in intellectual endowment, and that, while drinking means failure, abstinence is likely to mean success.

THE TWELVE STEPS[2]

Step One:

"We admitted we were powerless over alcohol—that our lives had become unmanageable."

Step Two:

"Came to believe that a Power greater than ourselves could restore us to sanity."

Step Three:

"Made a decision to turn our will and our lives over to the care of God as we understood him."

Step Four:

"Made a searching and fearless moral inventory of ourselves."

Step Five:

"Admitted to God, to ourselves, and to another human being, the exact nature of our wrongs."

Step Six:

"Were entirely ready to have God remove all these defects of character."

Step Seven:

"Humbly asked him to remove our shortcomings."

Step Eight:

"Made a list of all persons we had harmed, and became willing to make amends to them all."

Step Nine:

"Made direct amends to such people whenever possible, except when to do so would injure them or others."

Step Ten:

"Continued to take personal inventory and when we were wrong promptly admitted it."

Step Eleven:

"Sought through prayer and meditation to improve our conscious

[2] From *Twelve Steps and Twelve Traditions,* Anonymous (New York: Harper & Brothers, 1953).

contact with God as we understood him, praying only for knowledge of his will for us and the power to carry that out."

Step Twelve:

"Having had a spiritual awakening as the result of these steps, we tried to carry this message to alcoholics, and to practice these principles in all our affairs."

THE TWELVE TRADITIONS

Tradition One:

"Our common welfare should come first; personal recovery depends on A.A. unity."

Tradition Two:

"For our group purpose there is but one ultimate authority—a loving God as he may express himself in our group conscience. Our leaders are but trusted servants; they do not govern."

Tradition Three:

"The only requirement for A.A. membership is a desire to stop drinking."

Tradition Four:

"Each group should be autonomous except in matters affecting other groups or A.A. as a whole."

Tradition Five:

"Each group has but one primary purpose—to carry its message to the alcoholic who still suffers."

Tradition Six:

"An A.A. group ought never endorse, finance, or lend the A.A. name to any related facility or outside enterprise, lest problems of money, property, and prestige divert us from our primary purpose."

Tradition Seven:

"Every A.A. group ought to be fully self-supporting, declining outside contributions."

Tradition Eight:

"Alcoholics Anonymous should remain forever non-professional, but our service centers may employ special workers."

Tradition Nine:

"A.A. as such, ought never be organized; but we may create service boards or committees directly responsible to those they serve."

Tradition Ten:

"Alcoholics Anonymous has no opinion on outside issues; hence the A.A. name ought never be drawn into public controversy."

Tradition Eleven:

"Our public relations policy is based on attraction rather than promotion; we need always maintain personal anonymity at the level of press, radio, and films."

Tradition Twelve:

"Anonymity is the spiritual foundation of our traditions, ever reminding us to place principles before personalities."

4 The Ultimate
in Escape

On an eighteen-inch ledge seventeen stories above the street on the front of the Gotham Hotel overlooking Fifty-fifth Street and Fifth Avenue in New York, a young man stood for eleven hours of agonizing suspense. The date was July 26, 1938. The noonday business crowds on their way to and from luncheon spotted the man on the ledge. He was twenty-five years of age, of athletic build, and wore dark trousers and a white shirt. He had taken a stand between two windows that opened onto this ledge with sufficient space between them so that he could not be reached. If anyone attempted to go out the window after him, he threatened to jump.

Throughout the long afternoon and the evening and on into the night he smoked innumerable cigarettes, drank coffee, and waited. Down below in the streets a morbid crowd of ten thousand also waited—waited to witness the death of a fellow creature—as he teetered on the ledge one hundred and sixty feet above the pavement. One by one relatives and well-intentioned people went to the window and pleaded with the youth —his sister, firemen, policemen, psychologists, a priest from St. Patrick's Cathedral, the Deputy Mayor of New York Mr. Henry H. Curran, and others. While they pleaded, he quietly smiled but adamantly refused to enter the window. Repeatedly he said, "I want to be left alone. I'll figure things out for myself."

Some time after dark floodlights were turned upon the front of the hotel. A friendly patrolman implored him to quit the ledge. He replied, "I wish someone could convince me that life is worth living." Later he added, "I have made up my mind."

Just as preparations were concluded for two men to be lowered from the floor above and a cargo net to be lifted from below, he leaped to his death. Undoubtedly, a factor in his decision to jump was his statement that he would be "ashamed now to come in." He did not want to disappoint his public. This was his one moment of glory, with ten thousand persons avidly watching his every move. For once his uneventful life had come to public notice.

There are several aspects to this suicide that reveal important facts about a disturbingly large national problem. First: This man had a previous record of two attempts at suicide, one the year before his successful effort and the other only nine days before he jumped from the ledge. For a time he had been a patient in a state hospital for the insane. His case history underlines the folly of the saying that people who attempt or threaten suicide generally do not go through with it. As a matter of experience the reverse is true. When once the suicidal impulse has been manifested, there is constant danger that sometime the victim of this unnatural desire will accomplish his purpose.

Second: The calmest person in the whole episode was the young man bent on destroying himself. In most cases when the decision has finally been made, the would-be suicide reaches a period of great calm and sometimes makes careful plans for those who are left behind. An instance of this interlude of calm is seen in the businessman who spent a quiet evening with his family reading a magazine and occasionally engaging in conversation. Then he remarked that he had to go to the store to pick up a paper. When he did not return in two hours' time, a member of the family went out to see what had happened and found him in a closed garage dead from carbon monoxide poisoning.

Third: Of all the recorded statements of the youth on the ledge, probably the most significant was the expressed wish that someone might convince him that life is worth living. If a potential suicide believed in the worthwhileness of life, he would never go through with the act. In the case of suicide we have an extreme illustration of the inability to face life and the overwhelming desire to escape it.

Sixteen to twenty thousand Americans take their own lives each year. The number of suicides has steadily grown since the 1920's. The importance of the economic factor in self-destruction is markedly emphasized in the fact that while in 1928 there were only 4,779 suicides in the nation, in 1931, when the full impact of the depression was felt throughout the land, a record number of persons—20,927—took their own lives. In that year every twenty-six minutes of the night and day someone ended his own life in the United States. In addition to the successful suicides, there are at least twice and, according to some authorities, three times that number of attempted suicides.

It should be said at this point that practically everyone at some time has experienced a suicidal impulse. On one occasion a New York psychiatrist lectured to an audience of several hundred persons. In the course of his address he stated that most people at some time have thought of suicide. During the question period a member of the audience indignantly denied this statement and said that he for one was a decided exception and that there must be many others. The psychiatrist smilingly replied, "Well, we'll think of you as the exception that proves the rule."

After the meeting a large group of persons waited to talk with the lecturer. Near the end of the evening a man came to him and said, "Do you remember me?"

"I'm sorry, I don't," the psychiatrist answered.

"Well," he said, "I'm the man who raised the objection to your statement that practically everyone has thought of suicide. I don't know why I ever said that because for years this has been a major problem in my life."

Many of us have witnessed similar happenings. At the close of a sermon which I had preached in the Rockefeller Chapel of the University of Chicago, a man who identified himself as a college professor waited to speak with me. He said, "I liked your sermon except for one thing which ruined it for me."

I asked what that was.

"You made a reference to a young man who had thought of suicide," he replied.

"But that was just a passing reference," I explained. "You may recall also that I said he didn't go through with it."

"It doesn't make any difference," argued this professor heatedly. "It disturbed me because if there is one thing that is contemptible, it's a person who would think of ending his own life."

His voice rose in indignation and many of the waiting people heard what he said. I found myself wondering how many of them recognized the significance of this man's remark. Without the shadow of a doubt he was talking about something that had become a problem in his own life.

All potential suicides, like the man on the ledge, feel they are in a dead-end street or that life has put them in a corner from which there is no escape. Slowly the powerful "will to live" in practically all human beings becomes weakened and reversed.

CAUSES OF SUICIDE

Among the factors that produce this change is inability to give or receive love. Generally, the suicide is convinced that he is unloved. He is seldom likely to carry out the impulse if he believes that someone really cares for him and needs him. Similarly, if he has a passionate attachment to some person or persons, or even to pets, like a dog or a cat, or even to a house, or a piece of land, or a bit of scenery, or flowers or trees, these attachments will often hold him to life.

Another factor is the attempt to avoid disgrace or prolonged illness. A son committed suicide because his father had been sent to a penitentiary as a robber. The fact of poverty, unemployment, failure in life, the threat of arrest for wrongdoing, the fear of a lingering illness, an incurable disease or mental sickness—all these may be spurs to self-destruction. In many cases one reads in the death notice of suicides: "He had been ill for six months." "He was deeply depressed by a business failure." "He feared that he was going insane." "He never recovered from the death of his wife," et cetera.

Still another factor in suicide is the effort to save others from trouble and distress. Often a father commits suicide to leave his widow and children enough money to live on. This happened not infrequently during the years of the depression. One father, before he took his own life, set forth in detail the financial arrangements that should be made by his family when the insurance money was paid.

One will almost invariably find in cases of suicide an overt or hidden desire for revenge. There were instances during the great depression of a father killing his wife and all of his children.

That was his last defiant act against society. When a member of the postwar cabinet in the United States leaped to his death in Washington, he brought, as the victim knew he would, indignation and wrath on the heads of his detractors. Often, too, there is personal revenge, as in the case of the husband who, from California, telephoned his wife in New York. After telling her that she had ruined his life, he shot himself. It is not difficult to picture the anguished efforts of the wife to find out what actually had happened. A similar event was recorded in the newspapers with the husband telephoning from Florida to his wife in New York.

In a small American town a daughter had a quarrel with her father and left home. The father wrote her a stern letter and commanded her to return at once. A day or two later when he went out in the morning to get his newspaper at the door, the body of his daughter was lying on the floor of the porch with a note in her hand: "I have come home as you commanded me."

Imitation is another potent factor. When a man leaps from a high building in New York, the police are always on the alert because his act is sure to be followed by one or two similar cases. A New York newspaper carried the story of a Brooklyn man, twenty-six years of age, who committed suicide in exactly the same manner as was done by a man whose death was described in a detective magazine. There was even an illustration showing how the first man had died. The young man propped the magazine at the foot of his bed and with the aid of a mirror bound himself in exactly the same manner and watched himself die.

The power of example in self-destruction was graphically illustrated also by the police force in New York. The March 2, 1941, edition of the *New York Times* stated that two detectives had killed themselves within the previous twenty-four hours, bringing to 113 the number of police officers who had died by their own hand since 1934. This for a time was one of the major problems of New York municipal authorities.

PREVENTIVES OF SUICIDE

What can be done to alleviate this widespread and persistent problem in the life of America and other nations? With physicians and research scientists battling day and night to save life and to prolong it, an obligation rests on us to try to discover what it is that impels men and women to toss away this most precious of all possessions. There is little doubt that this shameful squandering of human life could be avoided if the pressures and abnormalities resulting in suicide were only understood.

In dealing with a potential suicide we should first endeavor to ferret out his underlying problem or frustration. When the will to suicide is powerfully expressed, it is usually best to seek a thoroughly skilled psychotherapist—a psychiatrist or a consulting psychologist. The handling of a potential suicide is too heavy a responsibility for a pastoral counselor to assume. Persons who appear fairly well adjusted may be tortured by underlying emotional tensions and frustrations. They may have an inner rage against life with its disappointments. The danger point comes when that rage recoils and turns inward with self-reproach and a desire for self-punishment. That desire may find fulfillment only in suicide. It is often found that the roots of such an inner problem go down into early childhood, and therefore great skill is required to deal with it. In every case of severe mental depression the danger of suicide is very real and such persons should be referred to a specialist in psychotherapy.

Second, we should give every possible opportunity to the would-be suicide to verbalize his troubles. Psychologists have often found that when an individual can put his problem—sometimes his proposed solution—into words, the very statement will bring a larger degree of self-understanding and inner release that may well be a substitute for self-destruction. There is no better therapy than an opportunity to talk without weighing words and without fear of being censured. There would be fewer suicides if there were more intelligent and sympathetic people willing to listen to the troubles of others.

Third, we should surround the potential suicide with an atmosphere of love. We should do everything possible to restore his self-esteem and self-confidence, both of which are usually shattered. What he needs is not primarily romantic love but the knowledge that he is truly loved and appreciated by some other human being. We should endeavor to create situations in which it is obvious that his help is needed and that there is a valid place in life for him. He must have help in establishing genuine friendships and be given opportunities to do things for others. In the case of an older person it is often helpful to supply him with a pet that can be his companion and on which he can bestow affection, but human love is the most powerful of all factors in giving to people a feeling of self-worth and significance.

Fourth, we should make every effort to provide some constructive and useful work for a potential suicide. The old proverb has much truth in it: Satan finds some mischief still for idle hands to do. Even more mischief may be done by idle minds in discontented brooding, overmuch introspection, and the development of destructive mental patterns. It must always be remembered that the tendency to suicide increases with age. An older person is more subject to it than a younger. Older people today are often rejected because of age when they seek employment or are told that their services are not needed. They develop a strong impulse toward suicide when they feel that all opportunities have gone, that all doors have closed in their face, and that there is nothing of importance left for them to do.

Fifth, we should be more sparing with censure and more generous with praise of those closely associated with us. Sometimes persons who are doing a thoroughly worthwhile job and are esteemed successful in the eyes of their fellows may in periods of depression think of themselves as a failure. This was true of a brilliant medical man in his forties who held several responsible positions in medical societies in the State of New York. Apparently in vigorous physical and mental health, he presided over a meeting of a medical society and set forth plans for the expansion of a nearby hospital. All of these were approved at the meeting. The next day, having given skillful care to his patients, he returned to his study, wrote a loving note to his wife and children, and then took his own life. It was evident from his note and other circumstances that he lacked the ability to meet the problems of life and had regarded himself as a failure. Relatives of anyone expressing such depressing views of himself and of life in general ought to be alerted to the danger that may be involved and bring it to the attention of medical advisers.

The most powerful preventive of suicide is a firmly grounded religious faith. Such a faith exercises a stabilizing influence on character. It brings inner peace and well-being and provides available spiritual resources when the hour of crisis comes. Historical evidence to support this statement is provided by the marked decrease of suicides in the Roman Empire after the advent of Christianity. Harvard's noted philosopher, William James, adds his impressive testimony. In his essay *Is Life Worth Living?* he discusses the problem of suicide. We are aware that this was no academic essay, for during his adolescence and early manhood he suffered very severely from mental depression and suicidal impulses. So acute was his distress from these causes that at times it totally incapacitated him. In January, 1868, he wrote to his friend Thomas M. Ward, "All last winter, for instance . . . I was on the continual verge of suicide."[1]

---

[1] *Letters of William James,* edited by his son, Henry James (Boston: The Atlantic Monthly Press, 1920), Vol. I, pp. 124, 125.

In his essay James refers to the pessimism that often overtakes men who are delving into metaphysical problems: "Too much questioning and too little active responsibility lead, almost as often as too much sensualism does, to the edge of the slope, at the bottom of which lie pessimism and the nightmare or suicidal view of life. . . . Let me say immediately that my final appeal is to nothing more recondite than religious faith."

I am convinced that no other consideration offers so powerful a reason for believing that life has worth and meaning as faith in a God who is not merely an object of belief but also a Reality to be experienced, who is not only Creator of the boundless universe but also a Friend beside us on life's perplexing pathway.

Edwin Arlington Robinson[2] pictures the bleakness of human existence without God and belief in immortality:

> And if there be no other life,
> And if there be no other chance
> To weigh their sorrow and their strife
> Than in the scales of circumstance,
>
> 'Twere better, ere the sun go down
> Upon the first day we embark,
> In life's imbittered sea to drown,
> Than sail for ever in the dark.

At this point, the words of Robert Browning are peculiarly relevant: "God pity all poor souls lost in the dark."

A few years ago the American nation was shocked and saddened by the widely-publicized and tragic death of a United States Secretary of Defense, to whom reference was made earlier. He had given of his best to his country and in return received villification and undeserved, bitter criticism. Unable to stand the emotional strain that accompanied his work, he suffered a "nervous breakdown." For some months he was under

[2] *The Children of the Night* (New York: Charles Scribner's Sons, 1905), p. 11.

the care of a psychiatrist in a Washington hospital. According to medical testimony, he appeared to be making a good convalescence.

On his bedside table in the hospital there was one book—a volume of poetry. A red bookmark made it easier for him to refer to his favorite poem. The author of the book was Sophocles, the Greek tragic poet. It is profoundly significant that before he flung himself to his death, the patient copied out a considerable part of one of the poems entitled "Ajax." It was written on the back of a Red Cross requisition slip and dealt, all too realistically for the patient, with the tragedy of wounded honor. The poem culminates in the hero's suicide. Let me quote one paragraph from "The Chorus to Ajax" which is typical of its gloomy desperation.

> When reason's day
> Sets rayless—joyless—quenched in cold decay
> Better to die and sleep
> The never waking sleep, than linger on,
> And dare to live, when
> The soul's life is gone.

What dreadfully inappropriate mental food was this for a man passing through a great emotional crisis! I can think of another Book that might have been on that bedside table. Had it been there, a tragedy might well have been averted. I refer, of course, to the Bible. The red ribbon bookmark should have been placed at the passage which reads: "If God be for us, who can be against us? . . . Who shall separate us from the love of Christ? shall tribulation, or distress, or persecution, or famine, or nakedness, or peril, or sword? . . . Nay, in all these things we are more than conquerors through him that loved us. For I am persuaded, that neither death, nor life, nor angels, nor principalities, nor powers, nor things present, nor things to come, nor height, nor depth, nor any other creature, shall be able to separate us from the love of God, which is in Christ Jesus our Lord" (Rom. 8:31, 35, 37, 38, 39).

These reassuring, glowing, hope-inspiring words are calculated to dispel earthborn clouds of darkness and reveal the smile of God.

There is a painful similarity in the suicide of the Secretary of Defense just mentioned and that of the Canadian Ambassador to Cairo who committed suicide by leaping from an apartment building. He had undergone severe humiliation because of the widespread publicity given to alleged charges of communism against him. He had been repeatedly investigated by the Canadian government and whatever may have been true of his student days, he was declared to be a loyal and thoroughly trustworthy servant of his country. He frankly told his wife and his physician that he was deeply worried because his government would be embarrassed by the renewal of these old charges, especially when relations with Egypt were badly strained. He felt that the future held no hope for him. He said he was beginning to think that suicide was the only honorable way out. His wife and his doctor did all they could to change the Ambassador's mind and to lead him into more constructive avenues of thought. A constant watch was kept over him and he was urged to go away from Cairo for a thorough rest. On the very evening on which this discussion took place the Ambassador and his wife went to see a Japanese film entitled "Mask of Destiny"—a philosophic and classical story of Oriental fatalism. The message of the film was very much akin to the mood of "Ajax," the poem read by the American Secretary of Defense before his death.

Inasmuch as the Ambassador had served in Japan and understood the language better than most of the audience, he realized the full import of the film's fatalistic philosophy. At the end of the show his colleagues say he was much more relaxed and chatted quite amiably with his family and friends. At the breakfast table the next morning he seemed to have shaken off all his worries and his wife felt greatly relieved. There no longer seemed to be any necessity for keeping up an unrelenting vigil on his movements. It seemed that the worst of their troubles was over. What the Ambassador's wife did not know is the fact that, as we have already stressed, a period of calm often comes to the would-be suicide after his decision is made. There is good reason to believe that the Ambassador had made his decision while watching "Mask of Destiny" and absorbing its fatalistic message. After breakfast he remarked that he would like to go for a little walk. Quietly and calmly he entered a nearby apartment house, climbed to the roof, and leaped to his death. The type of attack to which he had been subjected was inexcusable. At such a time one's spiritual resources are put to the test. The degree in which we lack an undergirding faith in God will be the measure by which we frequently fail in life's crises.

An eminent anthropologist, Bronislaw Malinowski, said some time ago, "Modern agnosticism is a tragic and shattering frame of mind." The reason for this conclusion is not hard to find. One of the truly overwhelming fears that assail the mind of man is that someday he may find himself absolutely and completely alone. It is as devastating as the belief that we are unwanted and unloved. It produces a sense of solitariness that is terrifying. This feeling oftentimes sweeps over those who have parted company with faith in God.

It does not follow that they immediately cast aside all moral standards. Their ethical roots are too deeply implanted in character to be lightly pulled up. Inevitably there does come, however, a sense of frustration and loneliness. The zest for life and the feeling of hopefulness and buoyancy depart and a kind of incurable sadness takes possession of them. This fact explains many of our modern tragedies. Take the case of George Sterling, the poet. California regarded him as one of her greatest sons.

He died by his own hand at the age of fifty-six. The day after his death an editorial appeared in *The New York Times* asking how one could explain such a tragedy. He was the idol of all his acquaintances, a man of wealth, social position, and immense popularity. Why should such a man wish to end his life? The editorial concluded by suggesting that there is no explanation, unless the psychoanalyst can find one.

We don't need the psychoanalyst to find the explanation. We need only to read George Sterling's poetry to discover that through it runs a melancholy strain of pessimism. It begins to appear shortly after his sophisticated friends led him to abandon his faith in God. You will find it, for instance, at the beginning in *The Testimony of the Suns*. His friend, Upton Sinclair, says that George Sterling's philosophy of life could be expressed something like this: He believed that the universe is running down like a clock, and in some millions of years the earth will be cold. "So," he asks, "what difference does it make what we poor insects do?" It is a perilous hour in the life of any man when he begins to think of himself and other human beings as "poor insects." Yes, this was the philosophy of George Sterling and it altered his pattern of living. Finally, surfeited with it all—lonely, fearful, and sick at heart—he brought his dreary existence to an end.

On one occasion during a radio address I made reference to Sterling's life as an example of the tragic results of the loss of faith. A few weeks later I received an understanding letter from a member of his family who said that the diagnosis was completely accurate, that when his faith was strong and vigorous he was able to face whatever difficulties emerged, but this inner resilience and strength seemed to have departed with his faith.

What a contrast to this is the faith that Christ inspires in man—faith in the trustworthiness of God and the friendliness of the universe; faith that life is meaningful and worth living;

faith that no power in heaven or earth can separate us from the love of God or pluck us out of the Heavenly Father's hand. This faith begins in venture, but ends in triumphant vindication. The assurance that we are children of Eternal love casts out fear and creates resolute personalities, for love comes walking hand in hand with courage.

I know two German pastors who suffered years of persecution and imprisonment under Hitler's regime. The marks of the ordeal are still on their faces, yet they emerged from it all with an unbroken spirit. How do we explain this miracle of endurance? Let one of these prisoners tell us. Here is what he wrote in a letter at the height of his ordeal. It was smuggled out of the prison by a friendly guard.

"I have a clean conscience before God and man; and then I am not alone, but am certain of the nearness and presence of the living God. . . . In the darkness of the night and in the loneliness of the cell God's nearness becomes almost physically perceptible to me. . . . In prayer one becomes calm, so firm, so confident, and at rest."

This is the love that casts out fear and that enables us to face life unafraid. It is this assurance of the divine presence and power that will preserve us from those black thoughts and that hopeless spirit that leads to the precipice of self-destruction.

A little earlier in this chapter we noted that one of the most powerful motives to self-destruction is frustration in love, the inability to give or receive it. One psychiatrist expressed it in this way: "People are led to suicide because they have nothing and nobody to love." This devastating factor was especially manifested in the life of a man whom we shall call Mr. Brand. He had important business connections and for a time was very successful. His name was known across the United States in certain realms of commerce.

The first time he came to see me he said, "There is every reason why I should be happy. I've had success in my business. That doesn't mean I have accomplished all that I would have wished, but my success has been much above the average. I have a wife and three daughters but I am not happy. In fact the reverse is true. I am decidedly unhappy. Most of my unhappiness is at home. I have a deep conviction that my wife does not love me and that she has caused the three children to withdraw their love for me also. When they were smaller, I used to receive all their confidences but that's past now. My wife takes not the slightest interest in my business and has no sympathy whatsoever for me when I face tremendous problems with half of my fortune at stake in some instances. She is interested only in spending the money I earn. I notice that now my daughters do not talk freely with me. They give me no confidences. They don't share their lives with me at all. This is tremendously frustrating. I don't mind telling you I've come to the place time and again where I have seriously thought of ending it all."

After I had seen Mr. Brand on several occasions I suggested that we might meet in his private office. I wanted to have a look at his surroundings. He readily assented and one day while we talked together he showed me shelf upon shelf of magnificent exotic flowers. He spent an hour every day caring for these plants, watering them, pruning them, changing the earth on some of them, putting others into larger pots, and so forth. His eyes shone as he talked of these plants and he handled them with great tenderness. I could see that he had found one object at least on which he could lavish his love, even if he were blocked in relation to his wife and children. It was soon evident to me that part of the reason for lack of affection on the part of his family was the businessman himself. We became close friends in the course of the interviews and though he did not belong to my denomination, from time to time he attended my church. This friendship meant a great deal to both of us.

Then came a summer when I had to go to Europe. On my return to New York three months later I received a message from Mr. Brand's wife. She was terribly agitated. She said, "Things have come to a dreadful crisis and I believe that at any moment my husband may take his life." I telephoned his office. Though it was eight o'clock in the evening he was still there. He had not gone out for dinner and was alone. I asked if I might go over to see him and he assented somewhat reluctantly. When I arrived I found him dreadfully depressed. While he had a genuine affection for me, his greeting lacked the usual warmth. As we sat together he was silent and I was greatly perplexed as to what I might say to him. Suddenly my glance turned to the plants and my heart sank immediately. The earth in the pots was dry as dust. The blossoms and the leaves had withered. This was a danger signal of the most critical order. Something had to be done and done quickly if this man were to be saved. Suddenly an idea came to me. Without saying anything to him I got up from the chair and finding a large paper bag on one of the shelves took it and began to pick off all the dead blossoms and leaves. I was thus occupied for nearly fifteen minutes and said nothing to my friend who sat dejectedly in his chair. When I finished pruning the plants, I worked up the earth in the pots. Then going into the adjoining room I found a large pitcher and filled it and began to water them. When half way along the middle tier, I became aware of a shadow, and turning quickly I saw my friend standing beside me. He had in his hand a vase that he had quietly filled with water and he joined me in my task. In that moment I believed that the situation had been saved. We continued until all the plants had been watered and soon they began to show some slight signs of life. We sat facing each other. Taking my hand, very quietly and sincerely he said, "Thank you. From my heart I say thank you. I caught all the overtones of what you have done. As I watched you picking off those dead blossoms and leaves, I knew that you were picking the dead leaves off my life. And like those plants, I feel that I have begun to live again."

In the interviews that followed Mr. Brand gained a much clearer understanding of himself and of his tangled emotions. A deeper faith in God and in the meaning of God's love, which he learned through an experience of human love, was a powerful aid in bringing understanding to both my friend and his family. He had been brought up by a stern, unloving mother. The simple act of love I expressed toward his prize possessions at a moment of crisis apparently broke the barrier he had built within himself in the matter of giving and receiving love. I had the joy of seeing the dark clouds completely lifted and love's sun shining upon Mr. Brand and his dear ones.

One of the passages of the Bible that this businessman frequently quoted is part of the fourth chapter of Paul's second epistle to the Corinthians: "We have this treasure in earthen vessels, to show that the transcendent power belongs to God and not to us. We are afflicted in every way, but not crushed; perplexed, but not driven to despair; persecuted, but not forsaken; struck down, but not destroyed. . . . So we do not lose heart. Though our outer nature is wasting away, our inner nature is being renewed every day, . . . because we look not to the things that are seen but to the things that are unseen; for the things that are seen are transient, but the things that are unseen are eternal" (7-9, 16, 18).

DANGER SIGNALS

To sum up, here are seventeen conditions that may indicate an inclination toward suicide. Obviously, any one condition must become highly exaggerated or several conditions must operate together before the suicidal urge becomes dangerous:

1. When persons find themselves in situations with seemingly no solution.

2. Persons suffering from periodic depression or severe middle-age depression are potential suicides.

3. Persons suffering from apparently incurable mental or physical illness or unrelievable pain.

4. Persons unable to give or receive love, who feel that they are not needed and not loved.

5. Persons who have lost the faith that once was theirs and now feel that life is without meaning or purpose.

6. Persons who are blocked and frustrated in life through their inability to get along with other people, including members of their own family.

7. Persons suffering from sudden financial or business loss and who feel it is impossible to recoup their fortune and are brooding over this fact.

8. Persons suffering from alternating depression and elation with extensive intervals of moodiness.

9. Persons preoccupied with suicide and making frequent mention of it as a possible way out.

10. Persons who are given to long periods of brooding over the injustices of life, with expressions of rage against persons who have injured them. Special alertness is demanded if there are signs of the rage turning inward on the suffering individual.

11. Persons who indulge a great deal in self-reproach, who belittle themselves and feel they are a failure in life.

12. Persons who manifest deep feelings of guilt and who, in great or little ways, are punishing themselves for wrongs that they have done.

13. Persons who are brooding over a disgrace that has come to themselves or their families, who take it greatly to heart and are depressed about it.

14. Persons, especially fathers of families, that are in great difficulty financially and who carry considerable insurance.

Watch for any tendency to use suicide as a solution of the family's financial needs.

15. Persons in a suicidal mood for some days should be especially watched if a calm, relaxed period follows. That may mean that the final decision has been made.

16. Persons who cannot express a deep grief for a husband, wife, other relative, or a dear friend, when the depressed mood and unrelieved grief continues.

17. Persons emotionally upset and full of resentments who are looking for a way to get revenge on members of their own family, employers, or other persons.

Some Facts About Suicide

1. A study of world-wide statistics reveals that between 250,000 to 300,000 persons commit suicide annually.

2. Between 16,000 and 20,000 persons commit suicide in the United States every year.

3. Approximately 1,600 persons die annually by suicide in New York City.

4. There are approximately 3 male suicides for every female.

5. The most frequent causes of suicide are financial reverses, unemployment, incurable illness, frustration in love, domestic disagreements, middle-age and other types of depression, insanity, defalcation and other crimes.

6. Destructive emotions that promote a suicidal mood are: remorse, revenge, jealousy, guilt, inferiority, hate of self and others, fear of blindness, insanity, and death.

7. As a rule there are fewer suicides in the country than in the city. City values and tensions are inclined to promote suicide.

8. An exception to this assertion is seen in the case of Michigan where the rural rate is considerably higher than the city rate. The explanation of this phenomenon is most interesting. Suicides

in Michigan occur chiefly in the agricultural counties of southern Michigan. It is said that the influence of the city and its tensions has reached out into these farming communities.

9. The urge to suicide increases with age.

10. Suicide rates are lower among Negroes than among whites in the United States.

11. The rate of suicide varies widely between countries and between sections of the same country.

12. Of the nearly 20,000 suicides in the United States, three-fourths followed previous attempts.

13. The danger period for a potential suicide is 90 days after the terrible emotional urge to self-destruction has passed.

14. A study of 209 resident student deaths at Yale University between 1920 and 1955 reveals that suicide was the second largest cause of death, second only to accidents. In nine American universities suicide ranks third as the cause of death.

Conclusion

The question may be fairly asked, if a suicide actually occurs, what may we say in the way of comfort to bereaved loved ones? To what conclusions should we come with respect to the future state of the suicide? Some branches of Christianity regard suicide almost as an unpardonable sin. Little differentiation is made because of the mental condition of the person who has died by his own hand.

Various faiths have taken every conceivable view of suicide, from recommending it to uncompromising condemnation. The faiths that have recommended suicide have generally been of a degraded form and the motivations which they approve are certainly not acceptable to Christian people.

Only four suicides are mentioned in the Bible—three in the Old Testament and one in the New.[8] None of those in the Old

[8] I Sam. 31:4,5; II Sam. 17:23; I Kings 16:18; Matt. 27:5.

Testament is expressly condemned. In the New Testament the fate of Judas Iscariot is veiled in mystery. Christianity, however, from its inception has set its face sternly against all forms of self-destruction. It is true that the New Testament does not expressly forbid it but the Sixth Commandment, "Thou shalt not kill," has been regarded as covering suicide as well as murder. Christianity's enormous emphasis on the unique value of the human soul is the basis of its opposition to suicide.

From the time of St. Augustine suicide was expressly condemned in the Christian Church. St. Augustine's reasons were chiefly:

1. That suicide is an act which precludes the possibility of repentance.

2. That it is a form of homicide, and therefore a breach of the Sixth Commandment.

But even St. Augustine had to admit the possibility of exceptions. Several Christians who had taken their own lives were officially recognized as martyrs because they died in order to avoid the possibility of shame being brought on the cause of Christ.

It is undoubtedly true that many people who have been sane through the greater part of their lives, may as the result of nervous shock, disease, grief, or shame become unbalanced sufficiently to affect their judgment in a decision of life and death. The charitable verdict of the average coroner's jury, "Suicide while of unsound mind," is without doubt true in a large percentage of cases. It is highly questionable whether anyone has a right to pass judgment upon a victim of suicide, for so little is know of the pressures, frustrations, heartaches, and mental clouding that caused the act.

The compassionate words of the Scottish poet Burns[4] have application here:

[4] *The Unco Guid.*

> Who made the heart, 'tis He alone
>   Decidedly can try us;
> He knows each cord, its various tone,
>   Each spring, its various bias.
>
> Then at the balance let's be mute,
>   We never can adjust it;
> What's done we partly may compute
>   But know not what's resisted.

At best we may leave this issue in the hands of a God who is perfectly just as well as loving and merciful. These considerations should be brought to the attention of persons who have been bereaved by suicide. Here too we may well believe that the words of Father Frederick William Faber are relevant:

> For the love of God is broader
> Than the measure of man's mind;
> And the heart of the Eternal
> Is most wonderfully kind.

5 From the Most High
Comes Healing

We are witnessing today a revival of interest in spiritual healing. We read of faith healing in newspaper and magazine articles. We listen to its strident appeal on radio networks. We view it on television. Here are the authentic words of one newspaper advertisement of a television healing program: "Actual miracles happening before your eyes. Cancer, tumors, goiters disappear. Crutches, braces, wheelchairs, stretchers discarded. Crossed eyes straightened. Caught in the healing line as they occurred before thousands of witnesses."

In the South and the Far West canvas tents holding ten to twenty thousand persons are crowded nightly by an emotion-swept mass of people. Little attempt is made to exemplify the pattern set by Jesus when he said to many of those whom he had healed, "See that thou tell no man of this." Today the motto is, "Tell everybody of this."

While undoubtedly many of the current professional faith healers are earnest men, there are also those who indulge in actual fraud. A notable instance of such fraud involved a highly publicized faith healer in Miami, Florida. Ten thousand people crowded into his tent every night to applaud what appeared to be remarkable healings. The most exciting incident of the whole series happened one night when a mother came with her little child five or six years of age. The faith healer declared that her daughter was unable to utter a single word and that this was a tremendous handicap. The evangelist took the little girl on his knee and prayed over her. Then he spoke a word and told the child to repeat it. To the astonishment of everyone the child succeeded in doing this. Then he uttered a second word and a third with similar success. The crowd, jamming the tent to its capacity, rose to its feet and cheered. A reporter of the *Miami Herald* was present and he made it a point to seek out the mother of the child and secure her home address. The next day he asked her for the address of the school which the child attended. He looked up the principal who directed him to the speech teacher. He asked about the little girl in question and the speech teacher said, "Yes, it is a sad case and progress is bound to be very slow."

"You mean to say, then," asked the reporter, "that this child cannot utter a single word?"

"Not quite that," said the teacher. "She has made a little progress. She can now say three words." And the teacher uttered the three words spoken by the evangelist, the words which all ten thousand persons in the great tent believed that the child had spoken for the first time that night.

The aftermath of some of these faith-healing missions has been pitiful, with many disillusioned and despairing people finding that the temporary improvement produced by emotional excitement did not last.[1] Undoubtedly, as in all such instances,

---

[1] Many statements are on record—some of them accompanied by affidavits—of extraordinary "cures" that took place instantaneously in an atmosphere of electric excitement. These "cures" lasted from one hour to as long as one week, when the disability returned in full force.

there were cases of illness improved or cured. So great is the power of faith that it will produce results at times under the most unpromising conditions. But many of these "healings" have no element of permanence.

It is true that our Lord healed men's physical and mental illnesses. Nowhere does he suggest that they should be passively accepted as the will of God. But he always put healings in a secondary position. His primary mission was to proclaim the Kingdom of God—the rule of God in the hearts of men. Apparently he regarded the public excitement over his healings as a hindrance to his primary task.

While I was writing this chapter a letter came to me from a woman eighty-six years old who had been prayed for by a highly-publicized healer. He held out such extravagant hopes that, when none of them could be fulfilled, she sank into despair. Now she writes that because of constant pain she is praying to God to let her die.

What makes the situation so confused and complicated is that these healing evangelists, however mistakenly, are concerned with a spiritual force that is undoubtedly real. Faith, especially if it be linked with God, releases healing energies that powerfully affect body, mind, and spirit.

However, it is important to ask how we are to distinguish between a misuse of faith healing and a truly Christian employment of it. One of the sure earmarks of untrustworthiness in this field is the refusal of the "healer" to submit any of his so-called "cures" for medical examination. One competent investigator declares that he could not find one of the leading and much-publicized "healers" who was willing to submit a case to a medical board. This is in striking contrast to the methods employed at the Shrine of Lourdes in France. There no case is claimed as a healing that has not been first passed on by a board of competent doctors who represent various religious creeds.

Many Protestant ministers seek a similar confirmation of spiritual healings.

The Christian Church must bear a measure of blame for the present situation. What has been one of the undoubted ministries of the Church in apostolic days and at times since then has been neglected or ignored and most pastors have stubbornly refused to recognize the importance of spiritual healing. Consequently, the healing cults have moved into the vacuum thus created by the Church itself.

Medical science, too, must accept its share of responsibility. During the first quarter of the twentieth century many medical schools were dominated by a spirit of materialism. This point was stressed by Dr. A. B. Bond of Philadelphia who, in an address to ministers and doctors, said, "When I went to medical school forty years ago, our anatomy teacher in his first lecture said, 'Man has a soul and a body. That's enough for the soul. For the next four years I shall be talking to you about the body.' " The physician added, "He lived up to his promise. We heard of nothing but the body."

There were also those, of course, who would not even admit the existence of the soul, who believed man to be wholly a creature of his natural environment, living in a mechanistically determined universe. Today all this is largely changed. In an address at the New York Academy of Medicine a prominent physician, Dr. Smiley Blanton, referred to the spiritual element in man and added, "There is something here above and beyond the test tube which must come back into the relationship between the patient and the physician." That "something here above and beyond the test tube" is freely recognized today by the best-accredited medical science.

Seldom has this newer viewpoint been expressed with such clarity and forthrightness as in the words of Dr. Henry Asbury Christian, for many years a teacher at the Harvard Medical

School. "The physician will always need the support of a true religion. A simple faith in God and in his ways should emanate from all true physicians. If he believes not, this will be impossible. The believing physician can often bring into perfection a cure not otherwise attainable. There is no place in this profession for the agnostic or the atheist."

In their ministry to the sick, pastors see the work of physicians at close range and often wonder if doctors themselves realize the tremendous psychological and spiritual impact made in the the sickroom by the personality of the physician, especially when he is a man of faith. Often in a home I have seen the darkness of anxiety pass and the light of hope dawn on the faces of dear ones when the magical words are heard, "The doctor is here." One of the great creations of God is the family physician. He comes into the home not as a stranger but as a friend known and loved by all. Sir Thomas Browne, seventeenth-century English family physician and author of *Religio Medici,* once wrote, "Oftentimes when I go to visit a patient, I forget my profession and call upon God for his soul."

In seminaries all across the United States and Canada future clergymen are being trained to utilize the immense resources of faith in their ministry to the sick. They are instructed not how to replace but how best to co-operate with physicians and surgeons, how to supplement such efforts with the undoubted resources of religion. There is as much difference between the disciplined and responsible efforts of a trained pastor who is dealing with the sick and the activities of commercial, sensational healers as there is between a trained physician and an African witch doctor.

It is a mistake to differentiate, as some are now doing, between so-called "divine healing" and medical healing. All healing is divine healing. Medical science and true faith healing are both of God. God is not more active in so-called spiritual healing than he is in any other means of combating sickness. Physicians are truly God's agents of healing, whether or not they acknowledge this fact. Even if they do not, their situation may be akin to that of King Cyrus, the Persian, who was a pagan. To him came the word of God by the lips of the prophet Isaiah, "I girded thee, though thou hast not known me" (Isa. 45:5). Physicians are girded of God even though some may not acknowledge him.

It is inspiring to think of the great pioneers in the realm of medical research: Pasteur, the founder of modern bacteriology, as great in faith as he was in science; Lord Lister with his antiseptic surgery; Sir James Young Simpson discovering chloroform; Jenner and his smallpox vaccine that has saved millions of lives; Alexander Fleming with penicillin; and other discoverers of antibiotics. So the record runs right down to the present day with the Salk serum for poliomyelitis. Truly all of these men, as agents of God, have driven back the frontiers of disease and death.

What has been true of medicine is true also of surgery. We see the surgeon opening the chest of a patient, performing a most intricate operation directly on the pulsing heart, removing diseased arteries and replacing them, and giving hope of renewed health and activity to patients who to all appearances were doomed to lifelong invalidism. The ophthalmic surgeon, by an operation of unbelievable delicacy, gives sight to the blind. The orthopedist in a hospital for crippled children molds and straightens twisted spines and limbs so that these little victims will not be doomed, in frustration and loneliness, to watch with envious eyes their more fortunate comrades at play. What are these men but agents of God bringing hope and healing to his children.

Little wonder that an ancient Hebrew Scripture declares that the physician is raised up of God for a divinely appointed task of healing: "Honor a physician according to thy need of him with the honors due unto him, for verily the Lord hath created him. For from the Most High cometh healing" (Ecclus. 38:1, 2).

At the same time we witness God's power at work in the prayer of faith. Here is an actual happening. A pastor is kneeling by the bedside of a parishioner whom he commends to the healing power of God. Medical science has despaired of saving the patient's life but the quiet, even-toned voice of the pastor quoting well-loved passages from the Bible has had a strange and unlooked-for result. The patient's breathing becomes normal. There are signs that he is coming out of a deep coma and returning to consciousness. His will to live is quickened and strengthened. In response to the spiritual therapy of Scriptures and prayers, healing forces of unpredictable power are at work drawing him back from the very gates of death. We are reminded of the now-familiar words of Dr. Alexis Carrel: "As a physician I have seen men, after all other therapy had failed, lifted out of disease and melancholy by the serene effort of prayer."

One of the unfailing characteristics of the healing ministry of Jesus is that it was directed not to isolated human ills but to the redemption of the whole individual. The entire personality was involved. A serious mistake is sometimes made by persons exercising a ministry of spiritual healing in that they are satisfied with the improvement or cure of an individual malady as an end in itself and unrelated to the character of the patient. A physical healing may sometimes be accomplishd while spiritual ills remain—perhaps deeply rooted self-centeredness or even moral failure. Luke, the Greek physician, gives us a typical illustration of Jesus' mode of healing. A woman creeps up behind him and touches the fringe of his garment. The medical men of her day regard her illness as a judgment of God. She is branded as an outcast, expelled from the Temple, separated from her family, ostracized by society. (In the 15th chapter of Leviticus, her type of illness is diagnosed.) But the doctors of that New Testament period were mistaken. Her illness was not produced by moral wrongdoing. Mark writes that she "suffered much under many physicians, and had spent all that she had, and was no better but rather grew worse" (5:26 RSV). When Luke records the same incident, he is more generous in his treatment of the physicians, but then he himself was a doctor! Luke writes, "She had spent all her living upon physicians, neither could be healed of any" (8:43).

When almost in the depths of despair, she hears of the Great Physician. His reputation as a healer has become known throughout the land. So the idea takes root in her mind that if she can but touch the hem of his robe she will be made whole. Resolving to put her hopes to the test, she joins the throng and works her way toward the Master. More than once just as she is about to touch him, a surge of struggling humanity sweeps her back. Finally, with a desperate effort, she reaches out a thin, trembling hand and grasps the hem of his garment. When our Lord turns abruptly and asks, "Who touched me?" the disciples regard him with bewilderment. They point out that he has been thronged by hundreds of persons, so why does he ask such a question? He replies, "Some one touched me; for I perceive that power has gone forth from me."

The woman tries to hide herself because she knows that she has no right to be in that throng. The ban of the medical men and of the Church is on her. Now in fearfulness and trembling she confesses all to Jesus. His reply is full of reassurance. "Daughter," he says, calling her by that tender name which would indicate her restoration to God's family, "be of good comfort, thy faith hath made thee whole; go in peace." Here was not merely the healing of a specific ailment but the gift of "wholeness"—the redemption of an entire personality.

PSYCHOSOMATIC MEDICINE

One of the latest developments of medical science is known as psychosomatic medicine. That rather formidable term is from two Greek words which mean simply "mind" and "body."

Dr. G. Canby Robinson of Johns Hopkins Hospital, Baltimore, explains the new emphasis in these words: "Man is a unity of mind and body. Medicine must consider this unity. Physiology, chemistry, and biology cannot alone or together explain all the intricacies of life. The disturbances of mind and body cannot be dealt with separately; they form two phases of a single problem."

Several important textbooks have been published recently on this theme. What illnesses do the authors of these books attribute as much to human emotions as to physical causes? They include peptic ulcers, high blood pressure, abdominal disorders, migraine headaches, diabetes, and even tuberculosis. Moreover, these physicians say that in the case of infectious diseases, the patient's powers of resistance are dependent to a large degree on his emotional state. So the mind plays a most important role in nearly every type of illness.

Dr. Flanders Dunbar gives a striking illustration of this fact out of her experiences at the Columbia-Presbyterian Medical Center, New York. An elderly patient was brought to the hospital suffering from diabetes. He was responding satisfactorily to treatment when one day he suffered a sudden relapse. There was a marked increase in the sugar content of his blood. The doctors were completely at a loss to explain this turn of events. His diet, medication, and nursing routine were all unchanged. Later they learned that their patient had just received distressing news by letter. The physical setback was induced by disturbing emotions that changed the chemistry of his blood.

As a consequence of these new insights, medical students are told repeatedly, "Treat the patient as a person"; for the most part, medical science today looks upon man as an entity of body, mind, and spirit. Psychosomatic medicine has come into its own.

Some years ago a mild sensation was created at a meeting of physicians in Cleveland when several doctors from the Colum-

bia-Presbyterian Medical Center reported investigations conducted there for ten years. Case studies had been made of fifteen
hundred patients suffering from various forms of organic illness,
their ages ranging from fifteen to fifty-five years. The conven-
tion was told that in 80 per cent of these cases an important
psychic factor was found and that there was no hope for full
recovery until this psychic factor had been adequately dealt
with. Such considerations, however, are now commonplace in
medicine. When illness affects the human organism, where mind
and spirit play so vital a role, it is important that the patient be
considered as a unit. We have physicians and surgeons to care
for man's body, psychiatrists to treat his mind, and pastors to
look after the well-being of his soul.

These three areas of man's life are never to be thought of as
watertight compartments, for they act and react one upon the
other. Any disturbance in the spirit of man will inescapably
affect the health both of mind and of body. This is also true
of either of the other two segments of man's personality. Leaders in both medicine and psychiatry freely acknowledge this fact.

This threefold interrelationship in the human organism was
a key to an understanding of the illness of a woman whom I
shall call Jane Marsh. The first contact I had with her came
through her sister who wrote me, "There are three of us sisters
who live together in our home. Two of us are widows and my
third sister, Jane, who is an invalid, is unmarried. It is nearly
two years ago now since she suffered a stroke which has left
her rather helpless. She moves around the house with great
difficulty. My other sister and I must help her to the table, to her
chair in the living room, and to and from her bed. It takes the
two of us to help her get around. Things have not been pleasant
in our home now for five years because of a disagreeable situation that arose through my father's will. Ever since he died
things have gone badly with us, and then three years after his

death my sister Jane had this stroke. The only thing on the radio she has taken much interest in is your program. She has been listening to it now for over a year. It has greatly impressed Jane. She now maintains very strongly that if she got to see you, you might be used of God to cure her illness. We have talked with our family doctor and he is quite agreeable for her to come in to see you. Please write and tell us when it would be convenient for you."

Three weeks later Jane Marsh and her two sisters arrived at the church house. She was a heavily built woman about fifty-five years old, and was seated in a wheel chair. She was badly crippled. She made no attempt to greet me and seemed a little sullen at first. I suggested to the sisters that they go to the waiting room while I talked with Jane alone. For a little while she was reluctant to discuss her situation at all. When I asked her to tell me something of the history of her illness, she began to upbraid her sisters very bitterly. She said that when her father died he left her only one hundred dollars in his will and gave all the rest of his possessions to her two sisters. There had been a good deal of antagonism between herself and her father and this was reflected in his will.

"It seems as though a curse of God has been placed on me," she said. "I don't know why he has been so unfair. It seems as if life has singled me out for hard knocks. My sisters have always enjoyed good health and they are perfectly well now while I am a complete invalid though I am the youngest of the three. Both of them were married and had husbands who were good to them. I tried to keep the home together for my father, and what did I get for it? He left practically all of his money to the two of them who have been off on their own. It is a terrible thing when a person has to live on the charity of others right in one's own home."

After the father's death the family relationships were tense with frequent quarrels about money. She had asked her sisters to give her a part of what each of them received but they declined, so she devoted herself to making life miserable for both of them. She had developed a hypertense personality and suffered from stomach ulcers and high blood pressure. She often had mild heart seizures after spasms of rage and resentment against her sisters and three years after her father's death came the stroke, which completely incapacitated her.

"God has been just as mean to me as my father was," she said. "He plays favorites too."

I suggested to her, "Suppose we leave God out of this for a moment. Let us revert to your relations with your sisters. A moment or two ago you told me that from time to time you had spasms of rage and resentment against them. How often did you have these?"

"Oh, some days I would have to put them in their place two or three times. They have to be told where to get off or I wouldn't get any attention at all. I guess I have had outbursts of anger at least four or five times a week."

"Has it occurred to you that one of the main causes of the stroke you suffered and the lack of improvement in your condition the past two years may be due to your anger and resentment?"

"Why do you ask me a question like that?" she said. "You are not a physician. What do you know about this subject?"

I replied, "I don't know too much about the medical end of it but I do have the authority of physicians for the statement that chronic emotional tension, such as anxiety and rage, may produce changes in the organs of the body and in the arteries."

"I don't believe it," she said. "I just don't believe it."

I excused myself for a moment and came back with a book entitled *Studies in Psychosomatic Medicine* edited by the well-known physician Franz Alexander. I opened the book and read her a paragraph in which were listed organic illnesses produced by emotional disorders. She replied, "That's hard to believe. I find it difficult to accept. I've got to think about it."

The time for my next interview had arrived and I remarked that I would have to give her an additional appointment. When this had been done, she said, "But why did you bring this book on psychosomatic medicine to my attention? I don't see why a minister has any concern about these things."

"Well," I replied, "when you come in again, we can talk some more about this, but may I point out to you that religion can accomplish a great deal by eliminating the emotional tensions that produce physical ills."

As her sister came in and wheeled her chair out of the counseling room, Jane commented, "This experience has been terribly upsetting to me and so many new ideas have come to me that I will have to think them over carefully. I'm rather sorry I came."

One week later when she returned for the second interview, she said, "I purchased a couple of books on the subject of psychosomatic medicine and have read them since I was here. I have learned some things that I had never dreamed of. Indeed, I think I have become a little bit easier to live with. In the past week I have had only a couple of outbursts against my sisters and I did notice that I was upset for several hours after each one."

"Have you come to any conclusions about your condition?"

"Well," she answered, "I have resolved that whatever the cost I must find a way to achieve self-control and to find some means of getting rid of the bitterness that has filled my mind and heart for years."

"That's where the Christian faith comes in," I said. "If you will let the love of God enter your heart, the expulsive power of this new affection will change you and alter your attitude toward other people."

"But how does one let God's love come into one's heart?"

For answer I passed her the New Testament, asking her to read aloud from Paul's letter to the Ephesians. This is what she read:

"Let all bitterness and wrath and anger and clamor and slander be put away from you, with all malice, and be kind to one another, tenderhearted, forgiving one another, as God in Christ forgave you. Therefore be imitators of God, as beloved children. And walk in love as Christ loved us . . ." (Eph. 4:31, 32, RSV).

When she had finished reading these verses, I said, "Tell me, what do these verses mean?"

"I guess they mean that we must let God have his way with us and let his will be done in us."

"Why does Paul say that we should put away bitterness and anger and forgive as God has forgiven us?"

"Well, I suppose," she said, "that we have all offended God so greatly that the offense against us that anyone may have committed is small in comparison."

"Yes, I think you have put your finger on the heart of it," I said. "Are you ready now to commit your life to God and to forgive others as God has forgiven you?"

After a long pause she replied, "Yes, I think I am ready now. I have done a lot of thinking and praying since last week and I am beginning to see the light."

"How do you feel now about your relations with your sisters and your feelings toward your father?"

"When I am honest with myself," she said, "I have to admit that I brought most of my troubles on myself. You see, I was a schoolteacher and had to give up my teaching to look after my father when he got older. I bitterly resented this and I made life as miserable for him as I could. I regret this now with all my heart. Then I repeated the pattern with my sisters. All my life has been full of what Paul calls 'bitterness and wrath and anger and clamor and slander.' "

"Suppose then you now tell God how you feel about it all."

In a deeply moving prayer she confessed to God her rebellion and anger and bitterness and malice and asked for his forgiveness and that his love might sweep these things out of her life.

"Now," I said, "I think you are ready for another step and I am prolonging this interview for that reason. In the practice of spiritual therapy, when we ask God's blessing on someone who is in need of healing, we do not tell God what we think he ought to do. Finite wisdom doesn't dictate to the Infinite, but I am convinced that something is going to happen in your life. Indeed I believe it is happening right now."

As we bowed in prayer I asked for God's power to flow through her body filling every muscle and bone, every nerve and sinew and organ with healing peace.

When the prayer was ended, I called her sister in and explained that I would like to see Jane for several more interviews but felt that real progress had already been made. As the sister came to take hold of the chair, Jane Marsh motioned her away and said to me, "Dr. Bonnell, take my hand, will you?"

I did, and gripping it firmly she stepped somewhat falteringly to the floor from her wheel chair, and supported only by my hand at her elbow she walked slowly out of the room. Those were the first steps she had taken in two years without being supported on each side by her sisters.

Three months later I received a letter from her sister which said, "It is almost incredible to see the improvement that has come in Jane's physical condition. She is only a minor burden to us now because she is moving about on her own a great deal. But that is not the greatest miracle that has happened in our home. It is the change in Jane's attitude. She has become understanding, patient, and altogether uncomplaining. Indeed she has been an inspiration to my sister and me and love now reigns in a home where hate abounded."

When I finished reading that letter, I said to myself, "Isn't this exactly what Jesus had in mind when he said, 'I have made a man every whit whole'?" Body, mind, and spirit is blessed and healed by the spirit of Christ. This in its essence is spiritual therapy. It is illustrated in the story recorded by Luke of a healing by the Great Physician:

On one of those days, as he was teaching, there were Pharisees and teachers of the law sitting by, who had come from every village of Galilee and Judea and from Jerusalem; and the power of the Lord was with him to heal. And behold, men were bringing on a bed a man who was paralyzed, and they sought to bring him in and lay him before Jesus; but finding no way to bring him in, because of the crowd, they went up on the roof and let him down with his bed through the tiles into the midst before Jesus. And when he saw their faith he said, "Man, your sins are forgiven you." And the scribes and the Pharisees began to question, saying, "Who is this that speaks blasphemies? Who can forgive sins but God only?" When Jesus perceived their questionings, he answered them, "Why do you question in your hearts? Which is easier, to say, 'Your sins are forgiven you,' or to say, 'Rise and walk'? But that you may know that the Son of man has authority on earth to forgive sins"—he said to the man who was paralyzed—"I say to you, rise, take up your bed and go home." And immediately he rose before them, and took up that on which he lay, and went home, glorifying God. [Luke 5:17-25, RSV]

In this notable healing Jesus demonstrated that only as a burden of guilt was removed from the paralytic could he be restored physically so that he could take up his bed and walk. Jesus was fully aware of the interrelations of the soul and body. He knew that a sick soul will produce a sick body.

Not only did he heal men and women throughout the whole of his ministry, but he also commissioned and set apart his Apostles for a ministry of healing. Luke, the physician, writes, "And he sent them to preach the kingdom of God, and to heal the sick. . . . And they departed and went through the towns, preaching the gospel, and healing everywhere." It is not without significance that the words "heal" and "health" occur seventy-seven times in the New Testament.

The central objective of the healing ministry of Jesus and that to which he commissioned his followers was not merely a matter of curing physical ailments. It is made clear in words which I have already quoted—"I have made a man every whit whole." He sought the healing and renewal of body, mind, and spirit.

A New York surgeon called me one morning to say that a patient of his, known to me, was critically ill at the Columbia-Presbyterian Medical Center. "This is the third operation he has had," explained the surgeon. "It has cleared up all the trouble and from now on he should be a well man. Unfortunately he is completely exhausted. He has spent all his physical and mental resources and has nothing left. I feel that you may be able to give him an incentive so that he will want to live." Early the next morning I walked into the patient's bedroom and found him too weak to show any sign of recognition. I took his hand and quietly gave him the information that the surgeon had given me. "The doctors tell me," I said, "that there is no reason in the world why you should not completely recover. Remember the words of Jesus, 'Have faith in God.' A group of our people at the church are praying for your recovery. 'Have faith in God. Have faith in God.'"

I was in his room for a very brief period, but as I turned to leave I thought I saw a faint light in his lusterless eyes which seemed to indicate that he had heard and understood what I had said. Three months later he greeted me warmly in our church. Now fully recovered and actively engaged in his calling, he said to me, "I only vaguely recognized you as you came up to my bed that day in the hospital. I felt that the ties that held me to life were separating one by one. I seemed to be floating halfway between earth and heaven looking back at myself. Somehow those words, 'Have faith in God,' gripped me, and I did feel a strength greater than my own coursing through me. It was those words and that experience that seemed to anchor me to life and restore my desire to live. So I'm here this morning to say thank you to God and to you for being God's agent in my recovery."

HEALING AND THE WHOLE PERSON

In the Academy of Medicine, New York, a prominent American physician told a group of pastors and doctors that modern medicine had too long concentrated on a study of the disease to the neglect of the patient. Now, he said, we take into consideration the patient and also the environmental and emotional factors.

As an illustration of the manner in which spiritual influences could be a definite asset in a serious illness, he described a case history from his own clinic. He told of a plumber who had come in with a serious heart condition. He was given an electrocardiograph and X ray examination. As a result of the tests he was advised to give up his work immediately and to avoid all exertion. The prognosis was exceedingly discouraging, offering little more than a life of invalidism.

About a year later the physician received a report from one of the caseworkers at the clinic that this man was showing great improvement, that he was doing light work without adverse results, and shortly expected to resume a full-time job. He was called in again, and the same series of tests was made. Said the lecturer:

"To our amazement, we were unable to discover the slightest symptom of the disease that seemed so marked twelve months earlier. I asked the man: 'What have you been doing in the last twelve months?' 'Well,' he said, 'the future didn't look very bright for me. I followed your instructions but since I had nothing else to do, I took up what I hadn't done for a long time. I began to read my Bible. As I read it, the peace of God came into my life, and little by little I found that I was improving. I have kept up the practice of Bible reading ever since.'

"We discharged the man as cured," concluded the physician. At the time of the lecture the patient was carrying on his normal occupation.

This is not an isolated instance. I believe that in the second half of the twentieth century one of the most important developments in both medicine and religion will be a recognition of the healing power of faith, combined with medical science.

Now, if this be true of organic illnesses how much more does it apply to those inner strains and tensions that incapacitate men and women. Especially the so-called white-collar workers are thus robbed of their serenity and peace. How often we hear it said, "My brain is tired from prolonged concentration on my work." But that explanation is no longer valid for physiologists now tell us that it is practically impossible to fatigue the human brain. So we are driven to find another explanation of our weariness. Someone is always robbing us of our comforting "alibis." How, then, are we to account for the physical, as well as the mental, exhaustion that often overtakes us when the only physical effort we may make is to sit at a desk for eight hours a day, with brief intermissions?

Let one of the better-known medical scientists answer this question. He says, "One hundred per cent of the fatigue of the sedentary worker, in good health, is due to emotional factors."

I have often noted that modern psychologists have seldom blazed trails that were unknown to Professor William James of Harvard. Half a century ago Professor James wrote this:

Neither the nature nor the amount of work is accountable for the frequency and severity of our breakdowns, but their cause lies rather in those absurd feelings of hurry . . . in that breathlessness and tension, that anxiety of feature, that solicitude of result, and that lack of inner harmony and ease by which the work, with us, is apt to be accompanied.

It is not our work that wears us down; it is the destructive emotional accompaniments of labor. The deadliest of all of these are worries, fears, and hates. It is probably more true of Americans than of any other people that we have never learned to relax as we work. As a consequence, we waste a great deal of energy which should be used much more profitably since every taut muscle is a working muscle.

In every walk of life, especially in our great cities, men and women return home at night worn with fatigue. In their intensity they have lavished the very marrow of their lives. The strain is killing. The pace is murderous. They are wearing themselves out not by overwork, but by destructive emotions manifested in unnecessary conflicts with other people, in worry, and in hypertension.

Feverish, distracted, tense living is, however, not a problem confined to the cities or the twentieth century. It has been true of every age. It is a characteristic of man's frailty. It was true even in Jesus' day.

On one occasion the disciples of Jesus returned to report to him the results of their preaching mission. They had experienced an unlooked-for success. The multitude, drawn together by the excitement, thronged them. Jesus looked at these fevered, tired, excited ambassadors of his and said to them, "Come ye yourselves apart into a solitary place and rest awhile." Mark adds, "There were many coming and going and they had no leisure so much as to eat."

He led his disciples to a quiet retreat. It was a secluded spot where, under the trees and amid the flowers and grass, they could meet together in fellowship with God and have their bodies rested and their souls restored. They had gone by boat across the Sea of Galilee to escape the multitude and there, amid the peace of nature, they sought renewed calm, humble recollection, and healing of soul.

Jesus wished to give the disciples something that all of us need, something that restores the balance between the inward life and the outward. Crowds and excitement and emotional pressure have the effect of externalizing our lives. The outer voices become so clamorous around us that we can no longer hear the inner, quiet voice. When, however, we deliberately come apart from the world, when the pressure of external circumstances relaxes and the veil that hides the eternal world from our sight is parted, we enter the holiest of holies. Then we know ourselves to be in the presence of God.

It is a law of life that retirement and silence are the secrets of productivity and strength. The only really strong people, the only truly productive people, are those who know the meaning of silence and solitude.

Thomas Carlyle, in his lecture "The Hero as Prophet," calls attention to the undeniable influence of solitude in fortifying the character of men and women. It was not an accident that Moses spent forty years in the wilderness as a shepherd. In this humble vocation, from out of those vast, unpeopled solitudes there came to him steadfastness and courage and faith. In the quiet of the night he would look up and see the stars shining in the canopy of heaven. They spoke to him of God's eternal sovereignty. Garrisoned in spirit, his gift of leadership now evident, he went back to take a band of slaves, soon to be liberated from Egypt, and weld them into a great people.

Far out on the Judean hillside a young lad was keeping watch over his flock by day and by night. There the silence of the lonely hills spoke to him of God. Eternal truths were nourished within him. Out of his aloneness came experiences and spiritual insights which enabled him to write incomparable poems known as the Psalms of David, poems that have been a comfort and a solace to men of all generations.

> The Lord is my shepherd; I shall not want.
> He maketh me to lie down in green pastures:
> He leadeth me beside the still waters.
> He restoreth my soul.

Such words as these, tradition says, were some of the fruits of David's solitude.

Jesus himself often stole away from the crowd and even from his own disciples into some natural seclusion for communion and fellowship with the Heavenly Father. When he returned from the mountainside, where on occasions he had spent a whole night in prayer, it is recorded that the multitude sought to touch him for power issued from him. He had become a channel of divine energy that not only made him invincible within himself, but that issued forth from him to bless and to strengthen other lives.

Illustrations of spiritual healing that defy a naturalistic explanation may be found in the life and ministry of many a pastor. An instance of this is seen in the experience of the Reverend A. B. Simpson, founder of the Christian and Missionary Alliance, which now includes fifteen hundred to two thousand churches.[2] He died in 1919. Dr. Simpson was born on a farm on the beautiful north shore of Prince Edward Island, Canada, in the parish which was my first congregation. He was brought up in a rather stern Presbyterian home. Early in life he showed great ability and when he became a Presbyterian minister, many predictions were made of his future success.

From a rather remarkable pastorate in Louisville, Kentucky, he was called to a New York church. He had been impelled to

[2] A. W. Tozer, *Wingspread* (Harrisburg, Pa.: Christian Publications, Inc., 1943).

leave the Presbyterian denomination and go out on his own as a free-lance preacher. At heart he was an evangelist. His great New York Tabernacle was crowded to capacity Sunday after Sunday. When he had been only a little more than a year in New York, his work was suddenly interrupted by a serious physical setback. He had had two previous breakdowns of this nature. The strain of his activities in New York had been too much for him. A heart ailment that had troubled him in the past was greatly aggravated and he seemed to be on the verge of nervous collapse. His physician predicted that he would have to give up the work of the ministry. Quite evidently he was sick in body and mind. His friends saw him from time to time walking slowly along New York streets old and tired, though only thirty-seven years of age.

In the summer of 1881, he visited Old Orchard, Maine, and there he moved about slowly in great weakness and bodily pain. His attendance at a testimonial meeting, where some people declared that God had healed their physical ills, drove him back to his New Testament.

One afternoon he walked painfully and slowly into a woods. On a carpet of soft pine needles he knelt by a fallen log and sought the face of God. Suddenly God's power touched his life. He said afterward, "Every fiber of my soul was tingling with the sense of God's presence." There he recommitted his life to Christ and the service of his Kingdom. He believed that God would give him the strength necessary for the task. Albert Simpson left that pine-tree temple a man spiritually and physically transformed.

A few days later he went on a long walk across country and a day or so after that climbed a mountain 3,000 feet high. When he reached the top, he said he felt as if he were at the gate of heaven and that a new heart had been put into his body. Never again through his long life did he suffer from cardiac disorders.

For thirty-five additional years he labored prodigiously in the service of Christ with abundant, overflowing health.

This experience of spiritual healing is strikingly similar to that of Dr. E. Stanley Jones, world-renowned missionary of India. When he first went to India, he suffered repeated "nervous breakdowns." Successive trips to the hill country of India brought no permanent improvement. A sick leave back to the United States produced no better results. It was only when he flung himself in despair at the feet of God that a permanent spiritual healing was wrought. He accepted the divine assurance, "Leave this matter of your health to Me," and in the strength of it he has labored unceasingly for decades in the Kingdom of Christ both in India and America without suffering a return of the physical and nervous condition that had previously disabled him.

This assurance does not mean that Dr. Jones takes unnecessary risks or that he and Dr. Simpson went through life on the strength of one spiritual experience. Both of these men of God drew day by day upon unfailing spiritual resources.

On one occasion Dr. Jones had been invited to speak to a Sunday night meeting of ministers in The Fifth Avenue Presbyterian Church. Six hundred ministers from all over the metropolitan area had gathered for the service. Dr. Jones's plane was more than half an hour late. He was rushed by taxi from the airport directly to the church and word was passed to me on the pulpit platform that he had finally arrived. I went into the church house looking for him but could see him nowhere. Finally I walked into the vestry, which was in darkness, and switched on the light. To my great surprise, E. Stanley Jones was lying on a couch in the darkness. I apologized for disturbing him. He replied quietly, "I am ready now. I had been so rushed I wasn't in fit condition to go into that service. I have been lying here completely relaxed and drawing upon God's healing power." When we went into the church and Dr. Jones addressed the meeting of ministers, I marveled at his quietness and serenity. He spoke as if this were his only engagement of the day and brought to all of us a realization of the peace of God. The power to mediate the healing peace of God is one of his greatest gifts to his servants, as many a minister can testify.

Word came to me one day that a parishioner was ill in a New York hospital. I learned from his son and daughter that he was suffering from a disease universally regarded as incurable. The children, in consultation with the doctor, decided that it would be inadvisable at this stage to inform their mother of the nature of their father's illness. She was not strong physically and the physician feared the shock might prove too severe for her, especially as there was a very deep bond of affection between husband and wife. After routine treatment at the hospital the father was returned to his home.

One Saturday morning at about eleven o'clock I received a call from the daughter to say that her father was dying. She added that the two medical specialists who had attended him had come in that morning and their verdict was that he would not likely last beyond one o'clock. She said she knew that Saturday was a very busy day for me and there would not be much purpose in my coming to see him as he had been in a deep coma for twenty-four hours. I told her that in any case I would visit him. Arriving at the home of my parishioner I found that the mother was prostrated with grief at this sudden turn of events. The daughter said, "I am sorry we didn't do more to prepare mother for this blow. All of us are afraid that she will not survive my father."

As I talked with her in the living room, I could hear upstairs the stentorian breathing of her father. Going up to his bedroom I was met by the nurse who said that he had had a nasal hemorrhage and that his body was swelling, which was one of the symptoms of the last stages of his illness. Going over to the bed I found his face turned toward the wall. He was breathing heavily. I took his hand and very quietly, but in a firm tone of voice, repeated the 23rd Psalm. Then I read well-loved passages from the New Testament that I knew were familiar to him and offered a prayer that God's healing peace might be with him in that moment. While I was offering the prayer, I noticed a change in his breathing. It had become much quieter. Pressing his hand I told him that I had come to have this prayer with him and assured him of God's presence beside us. It became evident to me that there were signs of returning consciousness. I told the nurse to keep watch on developments while I went down and talked with the mother.

On my return to the sickroom the patient opened his eyes and gently touched my hand. We had no conversation but it was quite evident that he was gaining strength. Before leaving I had prayer with him again. This time I was certain that he understood every word of this brief devotional service. By the evening he was completely conscious and for two hours talked to the family. The specialists were notified. Only one was able to come the following morning.

The daughter asked if there had been a mistake in the diagnosis as her father's death had been anticipated the day before.

The doctor asked, "What happened after my colleague and I left the house yesterday?"

She told him of my visit and the prayers.

He said, "I believe there was no mistake in the diagnosis but another factor intervened in the meantime—a factor that medical science is not qualified to evaluate."

Later that week when I visited their home, the father was seated at the dinner table with his family. There was no evidence of an actual "cure" of his basic illness but there was given to that family a reprieve of some months' duration that brought a rich measure of happiness to the mother and children, and prepared their hearts and minds in true Christian faith for eventual separation.

Ministers of all denominations, especially of the Protestant Episcopal Church, are becoming increasingly interested in spiritual healing. Dr. John Large of the Church of the Heavenly Rest, New York, Rev. Richard Rettig of St. Peter's Evangelical and Reformed Church, Pittsburgh, and Rev. Harry D. Robinson of Bellmore Methodist Church, Bellmore, New York, are a few of the many who have held or presently do hold regular services of healing. A flood of magazine articles and books testify to this growing concern in Protestantism as do the five seminars on Spiritual Healing held by the Laymen's Movement for a Christian World at Wainwright House, Rye, New York, in some of which I have participated.

Theory and practice vary, but the testimony is the same: Healing often follows prayer and the act of faith. Why healings do not always come or why they do not always seem permanent are questions impossible to answer. Yet we appear sometimes to experience eternity impinging upon time, to see the spiritual become manifest in the material, and so believe that grace supersedes law.

At other times, when conditions appear to be similar, healings do not occur. All of us who practice spiritual healing experience "failures" as well as "successes." But we are not to judge. As emphasized earlier, healing is not to be claimed as anyone's prerogative nor is it to be segmented. Healing and the healing of the whole man are creative acts of God, no matter who the agent may be. He who has healing in his hands, be he physician, surgeon, psychiatrist, pastor, or layman, may only thank God humbly that he is used in this ministry.

SPIRITUAL THERAPY

Here are some constructive suggestions to follow if sickness strikes us or a member of our family. Guidance is also offered on the matter of spiritual healing in general.

1. *We must never allow ourselves to become panicky.* Remember that profound dual resources are available to us: the skill of the physician, who will utilize the natural healing forces resident in our bodies, and the spiritual energies of the universe released by faith and prayer. Both of these are of God. Fear, on the other hand, impedes recovery.

2. *Call the pastor when the physician has been notified.* This chapter on healing testifies to the fact that there are powerful spiritual energies available to us. James says, "The prayer of faith shall save the sick, and the Lord shall raise him up. The effectual fervent prayer of a righteous man availeth much" (James 5:15, 16).

3. *In utilizing the resources of faith we are not to think that we are able to "use" God even for the noble end of healing.* Our objective should be complete and utter surrender to God and to his divine will. Only so can we become channels of his power.

4. *Beware of healing services that are highly charged with unhealthy emotionalism.* That is not the way Christ and his apostles did their healing work, and there is little evidence that God works that way today. Remember that God does not subject himself to the commands of men.

5. *No parishioner should seek healing as an end in itself and no pastor should encourage such an effort.* In some instances there are moral maladies behind the physical ailment, as was true of the paralytic borne into the presence of Jesus by four friends. Never lose sight of the goal always sought by our Lord: "I made a man every whit whole."

6. *When we have sought and found spiritual help, there are occasions when actual relief from a malady ceases to be of first importance.* Paul says that three times he besought God to remove what he called his "thorn in the flesh." This is believed by some New Testament scholars to have been a painful affection of the eyes, or recurrent malaria. But whatever it was, God said to him, "My grace is sufficient for thee: for my strength is made perfect in weakness" (2 Cor. 12:9). The apostle almost shouts his joyful discovery, "When I am weak, then am I strong" (2 Cor. 12:10). He triumphed over his weakness. He had learned, by the power of God, to live joyously and victoriously in spite of it.

7. *In the light of point six it is cruel and unchristian to tell a sick person that it is his own lack of faith that prevents a complete cure.* This type of irresponsible statement is the stock in trade of some "healers."

8. *It is especially important where surgery is indicated that the patient be visited by his pastor either the evening before or the morning of the operation.* The beneficent results which such a visit can produce have been noted by surgeons and anesthetists: the patient requires less anesthetic, recovers from it better and with less aftereffects; he is not so restless, seldom has postoperative fever; he goes through the crisis of an acute illness more easily, and has a quicker and less eventful convalescence. He will exemplify the words of the prophet, "In quietness and in confidence shall be your strength" (Isa. 30:15).

9. *Prevention is always better than a cure. Cultivate healthy-mindedness and maintain intact a devotional life that is renewed daily.* Keep inviolate a day-by-day appointment with God and his Word, a discipline to be outlined in the closing pages of this book. Be especially sure to begin and to end the day with him. This will prove to be an immense health asset. Don't allow such destructive emotions as resentment, anger, hate, envy,

unforgiveness, and self-pity to find a dwelling place in the mind and heart. As we open our lives to the healing peace of God, these minions of the darkness will flee away.

When you are ready for sleep, repeat quietly and believingly the words of the Psalmist, "I will both lay me down in peace, and sleep: for thou, Lord, only makest me dwell in safety" (4:8) and slumber will not desert your pillow.

6 Lives Remade

In previous chapters we have dealt with specific evils that threaten the integrity and well-being of people. Here we shall concern ourselves with the restoration and healing of lives that have already been disintegrated and damaged by life's encounters.

For three thousand years religion has claimed that human personality can be improved. Last century this affirmation was challenged and denied. A mid-Victorian critic of religion, Cotter Morrison, said, "Nothing is gained by disregarding the fact that there is no remedy for a bad heart." Other writers echoed his words.

"You can't change human nature!" These words have become a kind of proverb in our civilization. Let a group of people meet to discuss the economic improvement of the masses, education for peace, or the elimination of racial prejudice and hate, and someone is sure to say, "That's all very well, but you can't change human nature."

Now, in the twentieth century, comes the science of psychology declaring as an established fact that human personality

can be "formed, deformed and reformed." Actually, human
nature is the most plastic and educable part of the living world.
Of all creatures man is most subject to change. Heredity counts
the least in man while inner forces that make for transformation of personality count the most.

At the heart of the Christian gospel is the teaching that no
man or woman need despair, that there *is* a remedy for a bad
heart—the transforming power of Christ. Whenever Christian
churches and preachers have disregarded this truth, they have
become weak and ineffective.

Our bewildered, frustrated generation is hungry for a word
of assurance that life has meaning and purpose and that the
power of God can lift us out of defeat and failure and make us
whole. What limitless confidence in the Gospel of Christ is
revealed by the words of Paul: "Put off your old nature which
belongs to your former manner of life . . . and put on the new
nature, created after the likeness of God."

Human beings have a marked tendency to regard as an axiom
any saying that has come down from one generation to another. When it has become old and revered, it seems almost
sacrilegious to contradict it. Consequently, an untrue statement
may be preserved and repeated through the centuries. This is
exactly what has happened with this so-called aphorism, "You
can't change human nature." The statement is patently false.
In the experience of mankind human nature is one of the few
things that can be changed. The laws of the physical universe
are unchangeable. Man cannot alter the rise and fall of the tides,
or other operations of that mysterious force called gravity, the
rotation of our earth on its axis, or the laws that guide the
planets and the stars in their courses. These are fixed and permanent and will so remain until time shall be no more. But it
is quite otherwise with human nature. The deeply-ingrained
prejudices of men and women, the purposes for which they

live, their ambitions and loves and hates—all these can be altered, can be reversed, can be completely changed.

This possibility of change is of vital interest to educators. So we find Professor John Dewey writing, "If human nature is unchangeable, then there is no such thing as education, and all our efforts to educate are doomed to failure." The philosopher is right. The derivation of the word "educate" is from the Latin *educere*—to lead out, to bring forth, to inform, to enlighten, to indoctrinate, and all for the purpose of improving human beings. Yes, the educator knows from experience that human nature can be changed.

Again, the sciences of the mind are founded on the belief that human nature can be changed. What purpose would be accomplished by a patient going to a psychiatrist if he had no faith that he could be given new insights into himself and be led into more constructive ways of feeling, thinking, and acting?

Once more, Christianity has the greatest stake of all in the basic proposition that human nature can be changed. The Bible proclaims this fact from Genesis to Revelation. It is the central theme of every book of the New Testament. It is the heart and core of the Christian gospel. It is implicit in all the teachings of Jesus.

No one declared it more frequently than Paul, probably because he was speaking and writing out of an experience of dramatic personal transformation. The very fact that he was a Christian was in itself eloquent testimony that the faith of Christ can change a man.

One illustration of the strong emphasis Paul places on this truth is the verse, "Therefore, if any one is in Christ, he is a new creation" (2 Cor. 5:17). The King James Version says, "he is a new creature," but most of the new versions use the word "creation." Without a doubt "creation" is closer to the meaning of the Greek word used by Paul. It is employed in classical Greek to describe the creation of the world or the universe. Webster defines creation as "something brought into existence" or "invested with a new character." In other words, the apostle is telling us that when Christ comes into a human life, a revolution takes place in his personality. He becomes a different kind of person. His nature is changed. He is transformed. "He is a new creation." Creation is God's work. So John Wesley was speaking the sober truth when he said, "Only the Power that makes a world can make a Christian." So that no one will mistake the fact that a change has taken place, Paul adds, "The old has passed away; behold, the new has come."

A New Creation

What happens to a man who becomes "a new creation"? First, his pattern of thinking is altered. He looks out upon the world and his fellow men through the eyes of Christ. His attitude toward other people is changed. This transformation took place in all our Lord's disciples. Among them was one called Simon the Zealot. His name indicates that he was a secret revolutionist. He had joined with others to seek the overthrow of Roman rule in Palestine. We may be sure that he was one of the two apostles who carried a sword under their cloaks, and he would have been happy to use it to strike down one of those despised Romans whose heels were forever on Jewish necks. But when the Master was done with Simon, he looked through eyes of love upon these selfsame Romans and saw them as men "for whom Christ died." So also every racial bigot among these early Christians was changed into a true brother of humanity.

Jean François Millet, the son of a French peasant, caught sight one day of an engraving in an old illustrated Bible and was inspired to begin to draw and to paint. Through years of hardship and poverty and actual hunger, he continued to paint with pitifully slow recognition. Always his subjects were the humble peasants of Normandy working in the fields or with their flocks. He painted true to life, neither softening nor exaggerating what he saw, and the day came when people journeyed hundreds of miles to look upon these paintings. They saw these Norman peasants through the eyes of Millet, invested with dignity and nobility, the dignity and nobility of honest toil.

So it is with all who have given Christ the right of way in their lives. They look upon this teeming world of human beings through his eyes and they recognize no distinctions that did not exist for Christ. Their faces are lighted with a divine sympathy and their one endeavor is to make life a little easier for their fellow men, to smooth its rough places, and to lighten its heavy burdens. These are the marks of men and women who have become "new creations" in Christ Jesus.

Furthermore, the man who becomes "a new creation" is a transformed person. No better illustration of this fact can be found than Paul himself. Before his encounter with the Risen Christ on the road to Damascus, he was a divided and defeated self. In a bit of autobiography he tells us that he was powerless to do the right. What he wished to do, he could not. What he strove not to do, he did. His confession of moral defeat could be echoed by many a man and woman today: "I do the very thing I hate" (Rom. 7:15, RSV). Every counselor meets this.

On the day that Saul of Tarsus lay prostrate on his face within sight of the white-domed city of Damascus, he heard a voice saying, "Saul, Saul, it is hard for you to kick against the goads" (Acts 9:5). Into the mind of the persecutor flashed the picture of a maddened ox kicking against the steel-headed pole that prodded him. Here was an image of a self at war with itself. Never had he been able to blot out the memory of that regrettable hour when he stood by and saw the martyred Stephen die. He hated Christ and yet at the same time felt the mystic spell of the Galilean. Then came the moment of complete surrender with a glorious new light dawning on his soul, "the light of the knowledge of the glory of God in the face of Jesus Christ." Now his life is lived from a new center. "Nevertheless I live; yet not I, but Christ liveth in me" (Gal. 2:20); and there is a wondrous peace in his heart, "the peace of God, which passeth all understanding" (Phil. 4:7).

The life that began that day for Paul, however, was no parade-ground experience. Every day saw bitter opposition and conflict. Yet he could say triumphantly, "For the sake of Christ, then, I am content with weaknesses, insults, hardships, persecutions, and calamities; for when I am weak, then I am strong" (2 Cor. 12:10, RSV). Paul's life is a stirring example of changed human nature.

We should take note, too, of the important fact that *human personality can be changed at any age.* Often when this subject is mentioned, someone says, "You can't teach an old dog new tricks," and that's supposed to settle the matter. Well, that is possibly true of old dogs, but we are not discussing dogs. We are discussing human beings made in the image of God. From a wealth of material illustrative of lives changed after middle age, I choose but two.

The first is well known—that of Tolstoi. At the age of fifty the Russian author and philosopher underwent a thoroughgoing conversion. Later he wrote of this experience: "Five years ago faith came to me. I believed in the doctrine of Jesus and my whole life underwent a sudden transformation." In the last twenty years of his long life he was probably the most venerated person in the world.

The second illustration is taken from still more recent history—a man of our own time—the whole tenor of whose life was changed by a spiritual experience. Dr. Elwood Worcester tells of a fifty-year-old man who came to him for counseling. Despite his undoubted scientific gifts he felt that his whole life was a failure. His name was unknown, his works were unpublished, and his disposition was unsocial. He was a sick soul. This scientist came to a Christian minister for help and guidance. He was brought to Christ and learned of mighty spiritual resources available in him. His life was transformed and steadily developed in insight and power. The story of his achievements, in Dr. Worcester's words, "would seem like a fairy tale—were they not all recorded and dated in *Who's Who in America.*" A transformation of personality almost identical with this occurred in my counseling ministry during World War II.

This eternal truth of conversion Jesus pressed home on the mind of Nicodemus during their midnight tryst. As they talked, the leaves of the olive trees rustled in the breeze. "You hear the wind, Nicodemus," Jesus said. "It blows where it chooses. You hear the sound but you can't tell where it comes from or where it goes. So is everyone that is born of the spirit" (John 3:8, paraphrased).

How true that is. People talk learnedly of how all conversions should be sudden or gradual or should follow a fixed pattern, but Christ says that the operation of God's Spirit defies all our plotting and planning. You can't put God's work into a neat little formula and you have no right to try to run any man's life into the mold of your religious experience. It may be too narrow for him. God may have other plans in his mind for that person. This attempt is too often made by advisers and counselors.

William James gives an excellent definition of conversion that seems to accord with the New Testament: "A self hitherto divided, and consciously wrong, inferior and unhappy, becomes unified and consciously right, superior and happy, in consequence of its firmer hold upon religious realities."[1]

In varied ways men are ushered into Christ's Kingdom. Paul's

[1] *The Varieties of Religious Experience* (New York: Longmans, Green and Company), p. 189.

final change came suddenly. Peter's came slowly—with stumbling, faltering steps—and John's life was transformed not in a rushing tumultuous personal revolution but as gently as a flower unfolds to the light of the sun. "God," says Emerson, "enters into every life by a private door."

But back of all these special forms stands one fact that is undeniable: men and women can be transformed by the Spirit of God. There is a triumphant lilt in these words of the New Testament addressed to the members of a first-century Christian church: "Fornicators, adulterers, thieves, covetous, drunkards, revilers, extortioners . . . such were some of you: but ye are washed, but ye are sanctified, but ye are justified in the name of the Lord Jesus, and by the Spirit of our God" (1 Cor. 6:8, 9, 10).

No matter how great have been a man's failures and follies, his selfishness and sins of the past, he need not stay that way. The power of God can give him a new life for the old, a new nature for the old—a nature created after the likeness of God.

As Charles Haddon Spurgeon said one night to a congregation of five thousand crowding his great tabernacle in London, "Though thou hast raked in the very kennels of hell, yet if thou wilt come to Christ and ask mercy, he will absolve thee from all sin."

"Wherefore put off your old nature which belongs to your former manner of life . . . and put on the new nature, created after the likeness of God" (Eph. 4:22, 24, RSV).

THE MEANING OF CONVERSION

The word "conversion" is from the Latin *convertere* and means "to cause to turn," "to direct," "to turn about," "to turn back." It signifies a complete change of direction. It means that a life which was faced in one direction now faces the opposite way.

When John Masefield was fourteen years of age, he ran off to sea. In the wild and grimy life of a nineteenth-century seaman he met with many a sordid and seamy experience. His acquaintances at that time little dreamed that he was destined one day to become Britain's Poet Laureate. At the age of twenty-two he was idly thumbing through a volume of Chaucer's poems when suddenly his attention was arrested. One poem gripped and fascinated him. Later he wrote that it became "the poem of my conversion, leading me into a new glad world of thought, in fellowship with Shakespeare, Milton, Shelley, and Keats." Here we find the word "conversion" used in its secular sense.

"Conversion" is also employed in the sense of one's willingness to turn from deliberate sinning to obedience to the will of God. When it is so used, it views the experience of conversion from the human standpoint. It emphasizes man's part in this great transaction between a human soul and God. It signifies a fundamental change, with the consent of the will, in the direction a life takes.

On the other hand, when we stress, as we should, God's part in the experience of conversion, the more accurate word is "regeneration," literally "to be reborn." We use this word when we view conversion from the divine side. Regeneration emphasizes that this change in a human life is wrought by God and consists of his imparting his own character to us. A new life akin to the life of God is now begun. The results of a man's conversion are visible to his friends and neighbors; his regeneration, or spiritual rebirth, is visible only to God. Every counselor, and indeed every Christian, should understand this distinction.

When a man is converted and regenerated, it is often said that he is saved. Preachers and evangelists talk of the saved and the lost. When an evangelist asks, "Are you saved?" he means, "Are you converted to Christ? Are you regenerated, spiritually reborn by God's Holy Spirit?"

MISTAKEN BELIEFS ABOUT CONVERSION

Before considering actual instances of conversion, let us look at some of the errors that have crept into current thinking about this experience. *The first mistaken belief is that everyone must be converted or "saved" in the same way.* Such an assertion is false, as was pointed out earlier. Sometimes a preacher or an evangelist will describe his own conversion and imply that this is the only road by which men and women can truly find God. The result is that some people, especially young people, who have had a genuine experience of Christ will begin to doubt its reality and become confused and worried about their spiritual state. Jonathan Edwards, that brilliant and saintly soul of the eighteenth century, made this entry in his diary: "The chief thing that makes me in any measure question my good estate is my not having experienced conversion in those particular steps wherein the people of New England, and anciently the people of Old England, used to experience it." How pathetic! Poor Jonathan began to think that God dispenses his salvation only to those who receive it in the accepted New England fashion.

Let us never forget that God regenerates human souls with as many diverse approaches as there are individuals. The transition from darkness to light may be as sudden as a flash of lightning or as gradual as the coming of spring. Let no one believe that the eternal God has now standardized the manner in which he comes to men or that he authorizes anyone to compel us to conform to a particular pattern or to accept a smug little formula.

The second mistaken belief is that the moment of decision is of primary importance, while ignoring the necessity of a life-long discipleship in the school of Christ. The moment of surrender to Christ is important but it is not all-important. If the Christian experience is to be real, it must be transformed into

Christian living. This point should be stressed by counselors.

Now that word "save" or "saved" is from a Greek root *sōzo*. It is used in the New Testament in three tenses—the past, the present imperfect, and the future perfect. We are saved from the past. Its tyranny over us is broken. Our sins are forgiven. We have set forth on a new pathway. We are "saved." So Paul writes to Timothy, "According to the power of God, who hath saved us" (2 Tim. 1:8, 9). But the same word is also used in the present imperfect tense. We are being saved in the present. Paul writes, "To us who are being saved" (1 Cor. 1:18, RSV). Salvation is a continuous process. It is not static. It is moving constantly forward. There is also the future perfect tense of the word as it is used in St. Matthew's Gospel where he quotes the words of Jesus, "He who endures to the end will be saved" (Matt. 24:13, RSV). This is a reference to the final and complete salvation when we have grown into "the measure of the stature of the fullness of Christ."

Unfortunately, there are all too many people who are not informed of the wealth of meaning in that word "save" or "saved." This ignorance is the source of one of the greatest weaknesses of present-day Christianity. On one occasion I heard a man give a testimony somewhat as follows: "The red-letter day in my life is January 20, 1915. That was the day I was saved, the day I was born again. That is the day of days. It stands ever before my eyes." Even that patient and godly man Dr. G. Campbell Morgan grew weary of this kind of person. He described him as a Christian with one eye on Christ and the other on the calendar. One feels like asking such a person, "Did God go out of business on January 21, 1915? What have you been doing about your salvation ever since? What progress have you made? Have you grown in grace and in effectiveness as a witness for Christ and servant of the Master? And what are you planning to do in the future for him?"

The truth is that when we are saved from past sins and have undergone the experience known as a spiritual rebirth, we have made only a beginning. After that should follow a lifetime of spiritual training, education, and discipline. This is what Paul had in mind when he wrote, "Work out your own salvation . . . for it is God which worketh in you" (Phil. 2:12, 13).

Here, then, is a paradox—a Christian's salvation is already accomplished through Christ and yet he is to "work it out." This injunction does not mean that we earn our salvation. It is not achieved by our good works; the "good works" are an expression of the new life on which we have entered. They are the fruits of salvation and not the means of gaining it. Salvation is God's free gift to the undeserving. It is not something that we merit but something that God bestows upon us when we are contrite and penitent. We do not achieve it. We receive it. God bestows it upon us when we are most undeserving. So we Christians sing,

> Nothing in my hand I bring,
> Simply to Thy cross I cling.

Paul always carried this thought in the forefront of his mind. He writes to Titus, "For we ourselves also were sometimes foolish, disobedient, deceived, serving divers lusts and pleasures, living in malice and envy, hateful, and hating one another. But after that the kindness and love of God our Saviour toward man appeared, not by works of righteousness which we have done, but according to his mercy he saved us . . . through Jesus Christ our Saviour" (3:3, 4, 5, 6).

It is significant that, immediately after this glorious statement of salvation conferred upon the sinful and the undeserving, Paul adds this important counsel, "This is a faithful saying and these things I will that thou affirm constantly, that they which have believed in God might be careful to maintain good works" (3:8).

We are saved by the divine mercy and yet we must work out

our own salvation, remembering that it is God that worketh in us.

The fact that this important truth has not been properly understood has gravely injured the cause of Christian evangelism. Not long ago in a southern city I listened to a report made at a meeting of ministers. A series of revival services had been held in different churches in this city. When the ministers tabulated the decisions made, they discovered that in a number of cases the same persons had signed decision cards in several churches. They apparently thought they were being converted over and over again. They were living on the emotional excitement of revival services but did not go on to the development and nurture of Christian character. These persons are like a youth who will turn from one job to another but will not submit himself to the discipline of work and advancement in any one of them.

How true are the words of Beecher that "the church is not a museum for the exhibition of perfect Christians but a school for the education of imperfect ones." So it is—it is the school of Christ. The very word "disciple" is from the Latin *discipulus,* meaning "a learner." "Wherefore work out your own salvation, for it is God which worketh in you."

If this truth had been brought home more clearly to the consciences of tens of thousands of church members, we would not have on our church rolls so many static Christians. Not only so, but we would have less Pharisaism and less self-righteousness. Christians would be so busy developing their own Christlikeness that they wouldn't have time to pass judgment on their fellows.

A NEW TESTAMENT STORY OF CONVERSION

In the 19th chapter of St. Luke's Gospel we have a graphic illustration of what is meant by Christian conversion. On his way to the cross our Lord passed through Jericho. It was an important city of one hundred thousand inhabitants on the highway between Jerusalem and many strategic cities of the Roman Empire. Jericho was the bread basket of Judea, for the plains around the city were exceedingly fruitful. Figs, date palms, and other fruits were exported in quantity. One of the most valuable elements in Jericho's trade was an expensive balm which was sold in all the known countries of the world.

As our Lord was passing through Jericho, he observed a man, short of stature, crouching in the lowest branches of a fig-mulberry tree, right over the route where he must pass. His informant said, "His name is Zaccheus. He is a receiver-general of Roman taxes for this whole area. He's the most hated man in Jericho." As he uttered these words, his lips curled in scorn and contempt. The evangelist writes, "He was a tax collector, and rich." Enormous taxes were collected on behalf of Rome and out of them Zaccheus had unjustly enriched himself. As Jesus looked up into that tree, his eyes met those of Zaccheus and he saw the loneliness, the disappointment, the frustration, and the eager longing in the eyes of the tax collector. So he said to the man, "Zaccheus, come down quickly. I must have dinner at your house today."

Here is a startling example of our Lord's indifference to popularity and his disregard of the prejudices of the religious leaders and the people of his day. He knew that every patriotic Jew in the city would be outraged that he would go to the home of a "quisling" for the Romans—a man who was a traitor to his country and a renegade in religion. The people did not know that our Lord had come to seek and to save that which is lost, and Zaccheus was almost hopelessly lost.

But momentous things began to happen under that roof where Jesus sat at Zaccheus' table. When the meal was ended, and our Lord had finished his conversation with Zaccheus, the tax-gatherer accompanied the Master to the door of his home and addressed him in the presence of a huge crowd that had gathered in the street. "Master," he said, "I want to be your follower. I want to show my gratitude and love by serving you every day of my life. As proof of the genuineness of my profession, I will now examine my tax records and wherever anyone has been unjustly treated, I will restore to him not merely what the law demands, the amount that I filched from him, but four times that which I have taken. As an immediate proof of my change of heart I want you to know that I intend now to take 50 per cent of my fortune and distribute it to the poor of Jericho."

A gasp of amazement went up from the crowd. Could this be the man that they had known and hated through the years? It was the same man and yet a different man, for he had become a new creation in Christ Jesus. With glowing eyes Jesus looked upon Zaccheus and said, "This day is salvation come to your house." Not merely the taxgatherer himself but all who lived under his roof would be richly blessed of God.

Here is an example of a genuine conversion accompanied by regeneration or spiritual rebirth. This was no mere emotional experience but an authentic change of heart, a transformation that reached into every area of the publican's life. So every true conversion changes our attitude in each situation in which we find ourselves—the home, social life, business life, religious life. Our standards are cleansed and elevated.

What prevents so many people from experiencing this great blessing? The problem is not lack of knowledge. It is lack of a purpose and needful power. We are prevented by forces that are too strong for us from becoming the men and women we have always known we ought to be. We are powerless to help or save ourselves. Right at this point the divine miracle occurs. What we cannot do for ourselves, God can do for us.

One of the sins that may stop our spiritual advance at the

hour of conversion is self-righteousness. We have arrived. We are perfect. Instead of keeping the Lord ever before our eyes and seeking to mold our lives according to the divine model, and feeling the rebuke of his divine perfection, we begin to look around at our fellow Christians and question their sincerity and the genuineness of their experience. We become guilty of the blasphemy of usurping the functions of God. "This man's Christianity is true." "This man's is false. He hasn't had the experience that I have had. Therefore, obviously his religion is defective." "This minister's sermons are sound. He uses all the phrases that I use." "This man's sermons are unsound. He has a different approach from mine."

Have we never heard the stern words of the New Testament: "Who art thou that judgest another man's servant? to his own master he standeth or falleth. Yea, he shall be holden up: for God is able to make him stand" (Rom. 14:4).

The deadliest menace of self-righteousness lies in the fact that they who are mastered by it are the last people in the world to become aware of their own slavery. They are hampered, ineffective, crippled. So the prophet of God asks, "Who is blind as he that is perfect?" (Isa. 42:19).

Let us look away from our fellow men and cease to think that we are raised up to be their judge. This spirit of judgmentalism is a threat to the success of every religious worker and counselor. Instead, "let us lay aside every weight, and the sin which doth so easily beset us, and let us run with patience the race that is set before us *looking unto Jesus*, the author and finisher of our faith" (Heb. 12:1, 2).

Here are some questions each one should ask himself. "What next step in spiritual progress should I make in curbing my impatience? mastering selfishness? checking supersensitivity? overcoming moral laxity? Am I satisfied with myself as I am? With the help of Christ am I ready to take the next step awaiting me in spiritual advance? God put us into the world for a purpose. It will be unfulfilled unless we fulfill it. "Every man's life," said Horace Bushnell, "is a plan of God."

LATER ACCOUNTS OF CONVERSION

The New Testament is a long record of changed lives—men and women who came into the presence of Christ and became changed personalities. At least twenty-eight personal interviews of Jesus are recorded in the brief compass of the gospels. When we turn from the New Testament to the pages of Christian history, there is not a single century of our era that does not witness to some outstanding personality won to Christ, in addition to tens of thousands of less-celebrated persons. With some, the change was gradual; with others, it was spectacular and revolutionary. Let us consider three of these persons, all of whom tower above the men of their time.

The first is from the second half of the fourth century. Here is a young scholar, brilliant, winsome, profligate. In a garden at Milan he sheds tears of frustration and anguish: "O Lord, how long? how long? tomorrow and tomorrow and tomorrow? . . . Why not now? Why not this hour make an end of my weaknesses?" The sound of a voice breaks in upon his distress: *"Tolle lege. Tolle lege."*—"Take up and read." Reaching for a copy of Paul's Epistles he opens it and reads the words that first meet his eyes: "Let us conduct ourselves becomingly as in the day, not in reveling and drunkenness, not in debauchery and licentiousness, not in quarreling and jealousy. But put on the Lord Jesus Christ, and make no provision for the flesh, to gratify its desires" (Rom. 13:13, 14, RSV). Then followed the miracle of inward renewal—and the Christian Church had found a mighty advocate in the great Augustine.

The scene changes to the thirteenth century in Italy. A group of well-to-do young men are making their way happily and boisterously through the streets of one of the hill towns. They are going to a banquet hall to do honor to the most popular youth in the town. His name is Giovanni and he is a born leader. At the height of the feast they crown him "King of Revelers." But in the midst of all the riotous celebration, Giovanni disappears. His friends are bewildered. They can find him nowhere. He has disappeared because even in the midst of all his riotous living a divine disquiet has laid hold of him. Now he must make his surrender to Christ. When his friends meet him again, he is totally changed. They find him devoting his life to prayer and to the service of the poor. So Giovanni became one of the most lovable characters of history and his example and preaching instituted a revival of religion in Italy and won the hearts of all men. This youth, Giovanni Francesco Bernardone, now grown into manhood, as brave as he was gentle and compassionate, is known to history as Francis of Assisi.

Finally we turn to the twentieth century and see a young man nineteen years of age enrolling as an undergraduate at Oxford University. Before the year is over he has enlisted in the British army and is in the thick of the fighting in France. He is wounded and invalided to England. Now he is back again at Oxford. He has become a leader of the sophisticates, an emancipated, clever, cynical young agnostic. His chief joy is in casting sharp barbs of wit at Christians and Christianity. This brilliant youth has a large following among the students of Oxford, but the Hound of Heaven is on his trail. Twist and turn as he will, he knows that there is ultimately no escape.

> Still with unhurrying chase,
> And unperturbed pace,
> Deliberate speed, majestic instancy,
> Came on the following Feet,
> And a Voice above their beat—
> "Naught shelters thee, who wilt not shelter Me."[2]

[2] From "The Hound of Heaven" in *Complete Poetical Works of Francis Thompson* (London: Burns, Oates, and Washbourne, Ltd., 1913), p. 89. Used by permission of copyright owner, Sir Francis Meynell.

The crisis comes one night in Magdalen College. In his own bedroom he kneels in prayer and makes his commitment to Christ. Today Professor C. S. Lewis, author of eighteen books, the best known of which is *The Screwtape Letters,* is recognized as one of the ablest defenders of Christianity in Britain. He now labors to exalt the faith of Christ which he strove so long to destroy. "Therefore, if any one is in Christ, he is a new creation; the old has passed away, behold, the new has come" (2 Cor. 5:17, RSV).

Evidence of the transforming power of Christ in human life ought to be manifest in every Christian church as a normal part of its work. There is no more powerful and compelling answer to the indifferent world than this: a spiritual dynamic enters into the hearts of men and women and changes them in the very depths of their being. Even in that part of the personality which psychiatrists call the unconscious, where the impulses, drives, and motivations arise, there are unmistakable changes and spiritual renewals.

In apostolic days when Peter and John stood on trial before the Sanhedrin, it is recorded that the man who had been healed by the apostles at the beautiful gate of the temple took his place beside them. We read: "And beholding the man which was healed standing with them, they could say nothing against it" (Acts 4:14). Of course not, for they were witnessing the unanswerable argument for Christianity—the healed man. Similarly, as the churches of today produce healed men and women, they bring the best possible testimony of faith to an unbelieving world.

In recent years the Christian Church in the United States and Canada has witnessed the transformation of human lives as far-reaching as many of those recorded in the New Testament: discouraged men and women winning the battle at the very point of their former defeat, enslaved men and women mastering the appetites and passions that previously had mastered

them, frustrated men and women tortured by feelings of guilt
for the wrongs they had done confronted suddenly by Christ,
experiencing the divine forgiveness and going forth with the
peace of God keeping guard over their hearts. The transforma-
tions of human lives recorded in the Bible are all reproducible
experiences else they would have no value for us. They are
being repeated in our day. So shall the restless, confused, and
spiritually hungry multitudes, seeing healed men and women
appearing in the churches, not only be able to say nothing against
it but, persuaded by God's Holy Spirit, will turn their feet
into the way of God's commandments.

As one piece of evidence that human lives are being changed
in our time, I append herewith a statement exactly at is was
spoken by Gladys ———— to a group of some seventy ministerial
students and their wives from Princeton Theological Seminary.
Several of those who heard this testimony have written to say that
it will remain a permanent reminder to them of God's power to
change the most hopeless-seeming life.

Let us begin at the beginning as far as I can remember. I was converted just before I was sixteen and became keenly interested in
religious work. It soon became apparent to me that God wanted me
for full-time Christian service. Eventually I attended Bible School in
Toronto and after two years' study and graduation I went out into
the field. I always had the urge to be a medical missionary, and so
after two years of field work, I entered upon a nurses' training course
in order that I might better equip myself for the work which I felt
lay ahead. I did two and a half years of my three years' nursing training. In the meantime my family moved from Montreal to New York
and from the day they arrived things seemed to go wrong. My mother
was very seriously ill, my father lost his job, and the family savings
were wiped out overnight by the stock market crash. My sister, who
is eight years younger than I, was trying to keep things together. I
decided to go to New York to help out. I wondered at the time what
the outcome of this decision would be, but I hoped to be able to return
to my work or to get a transfer from Canada to a United States

hospital. This hope was never to be realized.

At first I affiliated with a religious organization, but I was never happy. I began to blame God for allowing these things to happen to my family and myself. Very soon I began to feel like a hypocrite. How could I say I loved God, when deep in my heart I bore a grudge against him? How could I sing "God is love," when I felt he had forgotten all about us? It wasn't long before I attended services less and less, and then stopped going altogether.

Always at the back of my mind was a verse of Scripture: "No man, having put his hand to the plow, and looking back, is fit for the kingdom of God" (Luke 9:62). That verse haunted me night and day until I began to feel that I was an outcast from God and society. Fear ruled my life.

This attitude of heart and mind didn't make for very happy living and little by little my health began to fail. My headaches were indescribable. If the doorbell rang, my heart pounded so hard it almost choked me. I trembled with fear when the phone rang, and I left my mail unopened for days on end. I was afraid of my own shadow.

Then a bright idea came to me. Maybe if I got rid of all my books and the things that linked me to the past, I might feel better. So one by one I began to dispose of, or to destroy, all the things I had used in my Christian life. I gave away my expensive books. I tore up examination papers of which I had been extremely proud at one time. As a last resort I gave away the trunk in which these things had been stored over the years. That afternoon I went down to Broadway, collapsed in the street, and had to be brought home.

Life was miserable indeed. I made two futile attempts to destroy it, to fling it away. It wasn't any use to me any more. Why should I continue living? I made myself desperately ill on these two occasions, but when I realized that I would recover, my bitterness toward God and toward life only increased. I hated everything beautiful and almost went crazy when spring came. I wanted to stop nature from fulfilling her mission. I felt that if only I could push the buds back into their tight little brown jackets, if I could just stop the leaves from coming out and the flowers from blooming, I would surely feel better. But springs came, flowers bloomed, and leaves came out, and I became more miserable. If any of you live in the vicinity of Central Park and have seen somebody walking there on a windy, stormy day dressed in an old raincoat and hat and rubber boots looking exactly like a tramp, in all probability that was I. It seemed a relief to be able to battle with the wind, to see the brown muddy earth and rain-swept rocks, to hear the trees moaning and see them straining and bending in the storm. I felt a strong relationship to all of this. It was a relief to see something else battling and to be able to battle something outside of myself.

About five years ago my health became so bad that I was constantly under a doctor's care. I was tossed about like a rubber ball from one doctor to another. Finally it was decided that I should be hospitalized to try to find out the cause of the terrific headaches from which I suffered and if possible to get some relief. After about ten days of tests the doctors decided to operate. They went into the brain at the back of the ear and all I got from that ordeal was a hole in the head, which I'll have as long as I live. Six weeks later I was doing the rounds of the doctors' offices again.

My personal physician then felt that psychiatry might help. He chose a very competent psychiatrist and put me in his care. We had a very stormy time together. I felt that whatever had happened in my past life was none of his business. As a result he couldn't get me to talk very much or to help myself in any way. He asked me on one occasion if there was anything that I felt would make me really happy and I said, "Yes, if I could just wring your neck and throw you in the corner like an old rag doll, I could walk out of here really happy." Of course, he didn't say, "Come on and do it," so I remained disgusted with myself and life and desperately miserable. I was interested only in living in a place of perpetual winter, with stormy weather and dark nights. I felt that I could wrap myself around with the darkness and that at least gave me a feeling of relief.

Then followed two series of shock treatments. They are pretty terrifying things to take, but even these I learned to accept as one more of life's miserable experiences. However, these treatments gave me an idea—whyever hadn't I thought of it before? It would be very easy to die by electricity. Criminals died that way, and what was I? The Bible says they that put their hand to the plow and look back are not fit for heaven—so what? I laid my plans carefully. This was going to be *it* and it should look just like an accident. Nobody would ever know the difference. I selected a Saturday when my sister was supposed to be out for the whole afternoon and started to prepare for the "accident" but she came home unexpectedly. She said she just had the urge to come home early. Had she not done so, it is very doubtful if I would be here speaking to you tonight.

Soon after this I heard Dr. Bonnell's Sunday afternoon radio programs. He asked his listeners to write him and let him know what they would like him to discuss that he might use these letters as a guide to the needs of his audience. That afternoon I wrote him a letter. Each week after that I listened, but he didn't discuss my topic or even come anywhere near it. I watched the mails for a few weeks and there was no letter from him. Finally I felt, so what? It's just like everything else, just one more disappointing experience. Then one day, months and months later, toward the end of April to be exact, a letter did come from him saying that he had been going through his mail and had come across my letter and that if I was still interested he felt he could help me. After a little correspondence we fixed the time and date. Thursday evening, May 5, 1955, at 5 P.M., I walked into his office expecting little.

He asked me some questions which I answered as matter-of-factly as possible and we talked for a while, when suddenly I felt I couldn't stand it another minute. I started to cry. For a long time there was no sound except my crying. Whether Dr. Bonnell was watching, thinking, or praying, I don't know. I was too busy wallowing in my own misery to care what he was doing.

Then very quietly and very slowly he started to recite Scripture verses, some from the Old Testament, some from the New. Then he came to the 103rd Psalm: "Bless the Lord, O my soul, and forget not all his benefits." Secretly I felt that I didn't have anything to bless the Lord for, and where were the benefits? But he kept right on. When he came to the verse, "As far as the east is from the west, so far hath he removed our transgressions from us," that verse struck like an arrow through my heart. He finished the Psalm, and as though he knew he had at last made an impression, he repeated that same verse over and over, "As far as the east is from the west, so far hath he removed our transgressions from us." Finally I felt myself becoming calmer. I stopped crying—maybe this is what I had been looking for all these years. Then with a sudden flash the whole panorama of twenty wasted years flashed before my mind's eye. I saw all the sin, the stubbornness, the bitterness, the suffering and the effort I had put into trying to run away. I thought maybe if I could get as far away from everything as the east is from the west, there might just be a chance that I could at least find a measure of happiness. For the first time in a long, long while, I smiled, because I felt relieved somewhat.

Dr. Bonnell seized this opportunity to say, "Shall we pray? Shall we tell God all about it—all about the terrible things you feel have happened to you—how you feel about him, and about yourself and about people? Shall we tell God all about it?" I said, "Yes, we will, but I want to ask you one question first. What about those twenty wasted years? What do I do with them? What do I have to do about them? What, just what happens to them?" He said, "Just let's take those twenty wasted years and drop them in the sea of God's forgetfulness," and that's what we did. Together we prayed. Then we came back to that verse in the 103rd Psalm and made it personal. "As far as the east is from the west, so far hath he removed my transgressions from me," and that night I became a new creature in Christ Jesus.

That was the beginning of an entirely new life for me. It hasn't always been easy. Don't ever let anyone tell you the devil isn't real. I know he is. I've battled him, but I haven't been in there battling alone, for God has been with me. My minister has been a constant counselor, helping and encouraging me when the going has been hard. I have had to relearn how to live, to learn again how to associate with and work with people. He introduced me to the most wonderful human friend I ever had in the person of Mrs. Betty ———. She too has had tons of patience with me. Through Betty I met Corinne, through Corinne I came into the sewing group, and through this group into the Professional and Business Women's group, and so little by little I have come to feel that, once again, I am an accepted member of society. You can believe me when I say it feels good.

Never shall I forget the first Sunday morning service I attended at Fifth Avenue Church. I wasn't prepared for such a large congregation. I went in the side door, looked inside the church, then walked out the front entrance, walked around to the other side door, looked inside again, and out again. I just couldn't imagine being among so many people. But I had promised to attend this service, so I had to keep this promise because Dr. Bonnell had said to speak to him after the service. Then I thought I would try the balcony. That was pretty full also, but before I could escape again, a young man came up and said, "May I find you a seat?" and before I could say "No" he marched to the very front row of the center of the balcony, and somehow I found myself following him. There I was plunk in the middle of everything. When we stood up to sing, I felt that twenty-four hundred pairs of eyes were on me. My head spun around like a humming top, and I trembled all over. When the choir sang the final "Amen," I must say I wasn't too sorry, and when I finally made my way up to the front of the church to speak to the minister, I was almost breathless. All I could say was, "Well, I made it." Nobody but God and I ever knew what a victory that had been for me, even if it had been a shaky one. But since that first service, this church has become a sacred place to me.

When I stood at the front of the church in the fall of that same year to be accepted as a member of The Fifth Avenue Church, it was the happiest moment of my life. I wanted to pinch myself to find out if this was really true or if I was dreaming. It proved to be true. *I, the one who had so wanted to die, was actually happy to be alive with a whole new life ahead of me.*[3] At the reception that followed I realized more than ever how good God had been to me, because by this time I actually had some friends and these friends really went out of their way to make me feel that I was welcome amongst them.

It's true I'll never be a missionary now, but I do feel that God still has some little service for me to do—maybe some little job behind the scenes that I can do with a smile. As the opportunity presents itself I'll try to do these things to his glory. My anxieties about the past are over now. The twenty wasted years have been dropped into the sea of God's forgetfulness. My concern now is to live for him one day at a time to the very best of my ability and to leave the future in his hands. I often use as a prayer some verses of the beautiful hymn which says:

> O Master, let me walk with Thee
> In lowly paths of service free;
> Tell me Thy secret; help me bear
> The strain of toil, the fret of care.
>
> In hope that sends a shining ray
> Far down the future's broadening way;
> In peace that only Thou canst give,
> With Thee, O Master, let me live.

The task of Christian leaders and counselors is not to help people either to adjust or to conform to their environment, which would often mean a lowering of their moral standards, but to

[3] Italics mine.

lead them into an experience of character and personality transformation. St. Paul has stated it concisely, "Do not be conformed
to this world but be transformed by the renewal of your mind,
that you may prove what is the will of God, what is good and
acceptable and perfect (Rom. 12:2, RSV).

7 Learning How To Live at Our Best

The man seated before me in the counseling room was dressed in a comfortable-looking tweed suit. We shall call him Frank. In every particular he was a well-dressed man but not overdressed. He looked like a man of energy and decisiveness. He had a kind expression that was attractive and reassuring. Nevertheless I knew that he was a failure. In the time that I had known him, some fifteen years, he had been engaged in at least half a dozen different business enterprises. All had failed. His problem was that he couldn't get along with other people. So far as I could ascertain, he had not one close personal friend, man or woman. He had never been able to adjust to others. A series of interviews revealed that, despite his pleasant appearance, Frank was a disappointed, frustrated, discouraged person.

First, he was disheartened and disappointed with life, for, while he had started out with high hopes, he had failed miserably to reach the goals he had set before himself.

Second, he suffered from a deep feeling of inferiority because he could not forget the fact that he had been brought up in a poor home. Throughout all his schooldays he was aware that his clothes were ill-fitting and of inferior quality to those of the boys with whom he associated. This inferiority made it necessary for him to win every argument and to come out ahead in every discussion. He couldn't bear to have his opinions challenged.

Third, he had become a disputatious individual. He was always critical of others. His stock in trade in all conversations was attacking the federal, state, or city government, the defects of the United Nations, the blunders of well-known statesmen. The world was out of joint. Furthermore, Frank was unhappy in his marriage. It had not brought to him the prestige he had looked for either socially or in the business world. Among his friends he delighted to tell jokes at the expense of his wife.

Fourth, he was emotionally immature. This made him ultra-sensitive to criticism. He constantly feared that his prestige or his authority was in danger. Daily he would have one of his sons or daughters "on the mat," lecturing them on the respect that they owed to their father, thus revealing his own lack of self-confidence and self-respect. Finally, he was not master of his own appetites and impulses. He was on the verge of alcoholism. When he became utterly cast down by some of these problems and frustrations mentioned, he would try to find oblivion in alcohol.

After an interview with Frank, I pulled down from a shelf in my library a book that deals with human relations. I wanted to be sure that the author had said that popularity could be attained by easily mastered formulas and techniques. All one has to do is to practice some simple rules and he becomes a thoroughly-liked person! How superficial such a statement is when placed in juxtaposition with this description of Frank and his problems. Except in the shallowest sense, popularity cannot be gained by any such means. It takes something more than pleasant manners, a good memory for people's names, and the ability to congratulate or flatter people to make one popular.

Everyone who lives to maturity is faced by a dual problem, that of learning to live with himself and learning to live with other people. These two problems are intimately related, but not until a man has learned to live with himself can he live sucessfully with others.

The measure of success that we have in mastering ourselves will determine, to a large degree, our ability to live happily with others. The person who cannot get along with anybody is invariably at war with himself. His impatience, his uncontrolled temper, his domineering ways are all projections of his own inner conflict upon other people.

Life is not an easy matter for any of us. It demands self-mastery. We must bring our own inner drives and desires and passions under firm control. We must discipline our emotions, establish constructive habits of thought and of conduct, and develop self-reliance and initiative. Truly this striving for inner unity is a tremendous undertaking—a lifelong task.

One of the characteristics of many modern persons is a lack of inner unity. Instead of orientation there is an appalling disorientation. "Disorientation" is a highly descriptive word. It means literally "to turn from the east"; in other words "to lose one's bearings" and by implication "to be confused as to the truth and the right." From the lips of young and old today we hear: "I'm so confused. I don't know what is right and what is wrong. I don't know where the truth lies." Every personal counselor hears people say: "I don't know what's the matter with me. I feel that I am going to pieces. One part of me stands aghast at what the other part of me is doing." This fragmentation of life is symptomatic of people who have no center to their existence. The centrifugal forces have taken over, the forces that flee the center, the forces that are disruptive and disintegrating. The reverse is also true. The happier we are within ourselves, the more harmonious will be our relations with other people. Each of us, then, becomes a center of discord or of harmony. Either we are making life easier for others or we are making it much more difficult.

A man in public life often marvels at the letters that come to his desk filled with hate toward other races and classes and persons. Most of the conflicts between people emerge from inner conflict and self-hate. When we have not achieved a self we can live with, we lack a self that others can live with. This thinly veiled, uncalled-for hostility between man and man is much more widespread than we like to admit. It is one of the symptoms of a sick society.

A precious stone, for instance, need not be studied in its relation to anything outside itself. The dealer in gems adjusts his magnifying glass to his eye and turns the gem over and over to detect its flaws or to enjoy the beauty of its flaming facets. But man cannot be studied in this fashion for he does not live in complete isolation. We cannot know what is in a man until we see him in his relatedness. Even in the case of nations, strained human relations are often a product of inner strife. A nation at peace within itself has larger possibilities of achieving peace with its neighbors. This is one of the reasons why China is a problem to the world. It is because of China's own tortured soul—unhappy, restless, divided within itself.

Our greatest ignorance lies in the relation of man to man and nation to nation. Many people simply refuse to try to understand; they are so thoroughly enamored with technological and material progress that they have lost sight of the desperate necessity for greater human understanding. Yet our material advance may even add to the human peril unless it be disciplined and regulated by moral and spiritual control. We may be able to split the hydrogen atom and fly faster than the speed of sound, but it will avail us little if we fail to bridge the yawning chasm between man and man.

The anonymous author of a jingle speaks a profound truth on the matter of personal relations when he writes:

> There's a fellow in your office
> Who complains and carps and whines
> Till you'd almost do a favor
> To his heirs and his assigns!
> But I'll tip you to a secret,
> And this queer chap is involved—
> He's no enemy to fight with,
> He's a problem to be solved.[1]

Whenever we meet with anyone who has not been able to achieve good interpersonal relations, who creates discord wherever he goes, we have "no enemy to fight with" but "a problem to be solved." And it is much more constructive to try to solve that problem in a kindly fashion than to start a private war. What a transformation would come in the human relations of any community if its people really tried to understand and help their fellow men. But that calls for a measure of self-discipline and inner peace that few possess.

Sir William Osler in his famous book *Aequanimitas* says that one of the first essentials to securing calmness of mind is "not to expect too much of the people amongst whom we dwell" and to exercise "infinite patience and understanding." How quickly our anger, our impatience, our scorn kindles against another! If we could only know the real heart of the other person, his problems, frustrations, and heartaches, we would soon let love have the right of way.

[1] James Gordon Gilkey, ed., *Meeting the Challenge of Modern Doubt* (New York: The Macmillan Co., 1931), p. 228.

A great many factors are concerned with our success in life. Some of these are beyond our control: the inheritance we have received from our ancestors, the kind of home into which we were born, the environment of our childhood—all these help to mold and to make us the way we are. Nevertheless, we are not the slaves of heredity or environment, and there still remains the one truly determining factor, the individual will. We possess the power, if properly applied, to make ourselves what we would be. God has laid upon each one of us the profound responsibility of being the architects of our own character and personality.

The proportion of people who really succeed in life, even in a material sense, is not large. Here are some statistics of insurance actuaries, verified for our day, on the prospects of any given one hundred young men in the United States who enter business at the age of twenty-five. Forty years later sixty-four of them will still be alive and thirty-six will have died. Of the sixty-four surviving men, only ten will be financially independent; fifty-four will be dependent on charity or relatives. These facts are disconcerting, but they happen to be true, and if one could go into the individual life of each of these men, one could trace the factors that produced the failure.

Even in the area of character and personality, the proportion of genuine successes is not much larger. It is not the many, but the few, who learn to live successfully. Jesus was aware of this: "Enter ye in at the strait gate: for wide is the gate, and broad is the way, that leadeth to destruction, and many there be which go in thereat: because strait is the gate, and narrow is the way which leadeth unto life, and few there be that find it" (Matt. 7:13, 14).

THREE REASONS FOR FAILURE

Why do so many people miss the straight gate that leads to true happiness, inner contentment, and the ability to live harmoniously with others? Why do they miss the abundant life?

One reason for their failure is that they lack purpose. Many young people fail in life simply because they have never made up their minds where they want to go. A youth without a sure purpose in life is like a rudderless ship at the mercy of wind and tide. Here are questions all of us should occasionally put to ourselves: Have I a clearly defined goal in life? Am I aiming high? Do I keep my main objective clearly in view?

Voltaire wittily observed of some of his fellow countrymen that they were like an oven that was always heating, but never cooking anything. Not so with Christopher Columbus! On his long voyage to the New World, each night he made one entry in his log book: "This day we sailed westward, which is our course." Hopes might rise and fall, the superstitious fears of the sailors might strike terror into their hearts, but Columbus, unappalled, made his unfailing entry, "This day we sailed westward." He knew where he wanted to go.

Paul had this quality of decisiveness in him. "This one thing I do," he once wrote, "forgetting those things that are behind, and reaching forth unto those things which are before, I press toward the mark for the prize of the high calling of God in Christ Jesus" (Phil. 3:13, 14).

"This one thing I do." Like Columbus, he knew where he wanted to go.

When a man has discovered a noble purpose in life to which he can devote himself, he should dedicate and concentrate all his powers of body, mind, and spirit to the accomplishment of this objective.

A second reason for failure is that many people lack the ability to see life through to a good finish. They have no staying power. They made a good beginning, but they can't see it through to the end. They are like the one of whom Jesus told: "This man began to build, and was not able to finish" (Luke 14:30).

A great deal has been said about the crucial years of youth and their influence on success or failure, but the experiences of life have convinced me that there is another period of life which is of equal or even greater importance—the years between forty and fifty-five. A depressing philosophy has been formulated for these years: "Too young to fail and yet too old to succeed."

Many people make a spectacular beginning in life. They are like a ship at its launching, decorated with bunting and with all the flags flying. Unfortunately, however, at the first taste of success and the first sight of their goal, they begin to slow down, to turn aside, to falter. The long, hard struggle with adversity has tested and refined their character, but now that success is on the horizon, their moral deterioration begins.

Watch those years from forty to fifty-five! "Too young to fail and yet too old to succeed!"

What has happened to such people? Why have their moral muscles gone soft? They have lacked great resources from which to draw inner strength.

Toward the end of his long pilgrimage, Paul said, "I have not been disobedient unto the heavenly vision" (Acts 26:19). He had not lost sight of his goal. Even while he was languishing in a Roman prison waiting for the heavy tread of the executioner outside the door of his narrow cell and for the rasping sound of the bolt being drawn ere he was led to his doom, he sent forth an exhilarating message of hope and confidence. In that dread hour he wrote as his last testament to his young friend Timothy, "I have fought a good fight, I have finished my course, I have kept the faith" (2 Tim. 4:7). The apostle's morale was unimpaired, his hopes were undimmed, and his courage never faltered.

True courage doesn't advertise itself; it doesn't boast of its deeds; it is quiet, strong, unobtrusive. Recently I was privileged to participate in a service of recognition for a group of naval and air men who had returned from the Pacific. One of them received the Congressional Medal of Honor for his exploits in rescuing imperiled comrades and going beyond the call of duty in saving the day for his unit. His was a distinguished record. I studied the face of this youth standing a few feet away. He looked like an average American boy. I was deeply moved, however, to observe that when the military choir stood and sang of the valor of the men who fought for freedom, the eyes of the young hero were flooded with tears. His thoughts were filled with memories of his comrades who never would return. This is courage at its best—masculine, robust and yet tender and compassionate. This is the courage that attains its goal.

A third reason for failure is that many people do not seriously endeavor to rid themselves of their faults. It will assist us materially if we begin our self-examination with the clear understanding of a fact known to spiritually-minded people everywhere and confirmed by modern psychology. Practically every character or personality defect has its origin in self-centeredness or, as the psychologists call it, "egocentricity."

Let us examine the truth of this statement. Take the hypersensitive individual, for instance. Sensitiveness is a desirable spiritual quality. Without it we should have no appreciation of art or of music or of literature; lacking it, we should not know the uplift of a service of worship. Nevertheless, as the Roman proverb puts it, "The corruption of the best is the worst," and sensitiveness can be corrupted and debased. When this occurs we become touchy and peevish, with a hair-trigger temperament; we are easily offended; we are readily hurt; we are often antagonized; we fly to pieces at minor irritations. We feel that our contribution to life is never fully appreciated. The explanation of this type of reaction is egocentricity, or self-centeredness.

If we are interested in tracking down our hypersensitiveness, let us take particular notice of the thing that annoys us most of all, the thing about which we are most touchy, and we will learn a lot about ourselves. Always it goes back to the source or fountainhead described by a word of four letters, "s-e-l-f." Self is enthroned; self is worshiped; self is defended; self is protected; self everywhere, self! So our Lord said that when we try to save ourselves, we perish. Only as we are willing to die to self do we begin truly to live.

What is the remedy for self-centeredness? It is old and yet forever new. Put self out of the center of life and enthrone God's will there. When our first concern is for him and the advancement of his Kingdom and obedience to his commandments, the greatest of which is to love one another, the little exasperations of life cease to irritate us and our hearts become homes of peace and of love.

Hypersensitiveness is a character defect springing from egocentricity. So is jealousy. Jealousy is "sensitiveness twisted into peevishness." It refuses to allow to others the satisfactions and successes we seek for ourselves. It is the rare and unusual person who will admit even to himself the supremacy of a competitor. Goethe said: "The only remedy for the superiority of another is love."

There is also anger. Track it to its source and we will discover that anger is generally caused by a sense of frustration within ourselves which we project upon other people. Much of the corporal punishment of children in homes and in schools has a similar origin. Something has annoyed the parent or the teacher, and the child has touched off the emotional explosion. An outburst of anger may afford a sense of relief at the moment, but we pay a heavy price for it in the loss of personal stability and general well-being.

Another character defect bred by egocentricity is vindictiveness and grudge-bearing, which always dwarf and stunt and shrivel character. These spring from wounded self-esteem and, when nourished, end in the most deadly of all emotions—self-pity.

Finally there is lack of consideration for the rights and feelings of others. This character defect marks the point where most friendships founder. It is also the rock on which many marriages are wrecked. The true explanation is most often not some subtle psychological factor, but just downright selfishness. The egocentric individual must have his or her own way at whatever cost. The irrefutable truth is that all of us have more or less of this destructive egocentricity in us. How many tragedies could be avoided in life if we remembered that other people too have a longing for success, a desire for appreciation, a hunger for a little happiness? They also have their worries and their heartaches, their hopes and their fears, their joys and their sorrows.

Frequently the reason we are annoyed by someone is that we possess in us that same irritating quality that we see in him. A dependable test of our defects is to observe the things that irritate us most in others, for these are likely to be our own secret faults. When we condemn them in others, we are trying unconsciously to subdue them in ourselves.

Of the thousands of choice quotations accumulated in a lifetime of reading, my favorite is a single sentence from the pen of Ian Maclaren, "Let us be kind to one another, for most of us are fighting a hard battle." This would make an excellent motto on a business desk or a bedroom bureau. We are fully aware of our own struggle but are often blind to the battle that others have to fight. These words plumb the deeps of human life, and through them shines the radiant spirit of Christ.

"Who can understand his errors? cleanse thou me from secret faults," says the Psalmist (19:12). How may we correct these defects hidden deep within us? By enthroning God in the inner life, where self has reigned too long. When his spirit takes possession of us we become free from enslavement to self. "Where the Spirit of the Lord is, there is liberty" (2 Cor. 3:17). Then the anger, the vindictiveness, the pride, the jealousy, the feeling of persecution, the hypersensitiveness, the inconsiderateness, the worry, and the fear vanish from our lives even as the darkness flees when we roll up the window shades and let the sunshine flood a room. When these evil spirits have fled, then hope, trust, courage, serenity, kindliness, and love dwell within. We can be rid of our faults if we submit ourselves to the Great Physician of souls.

Recall how John Bunyan put it. Emmanuel had driven Diabolus out of the city of Mansoul. Diabolus preferred a petition that he might be allowed to dwell in a small part of the city. When it was refused, he presented a second petition that he might be given just a little room within the walls. Emmanuel answered that he should be given no place at all, "Not so much as to rest the sole of his foot."

When God enters a human life, he comes to reign. The government must rest on his shoulders. He brooks no divided allegiance. When we are Christ-mastered, we achieve self-mastery and inner freedom.

> Make me a captive, Lord
> And then I shall be free,
> Force me to render up my sword
> And I shall conqueror be.[2]

Steps in Self-Improvement

The most difficult task in the world for the average man and woman is to look objectively at himself or herself. We all dis-

[2] George Matheson.

like to face ourselves. It is hard to be honest at this point. An understanding psychiatrist penned this sentence: "It is much more pleasant to feel a righteous indignation at others than to face a problem of one's own." Of course, the simplest way to avoid self-criticism is to discover and to denounce the faults of others. But we have not advanced far in spiritual development until we have sufficient courage to face ourselves.

I suggest six stepping-stones to self-improvement.

First: We should all be willing to admit that we have weaknesses in our character as well as strength. Someone says, "We all do that now." Do we? I wonder. For instance, every time we judge and condemn a fellow creature, as we frequently do, we are by implication telling ourselves what fine people we are. One man said, "I know I am right, but it is hard to make other people see it."

The greatest personalities of the race, for the most part, have been humble, teachable men. Sainte-Beuve, the French author and critic observed that "One can get to the very depths of human life without going outside of oneself." And Dr. Carl G. Jung said, "Every man has within him something of the criminal, the genius, and the saint." Mark Twain wrote that every year he lived he was more convinced that he and other men were alike. Whatever virtues he had were shared by others, and their vices in some measure were found in him.

On one occasion Paul swept with a glance those who boasted that they kept the law and those who admitted that they had broken it. "There is no difference," he said, "for all have sinned and come short of the glory of God." We manifest the spirit of humility when we admit our kinship with sinning, blundering, faltering men and women. It marks our first step on the upward pathway. When we flatter ourselves that we are so much better than our fellow men, our spiritual poverty is revealed.

Throughout the whole of Christian history only One could truthfully say of his relations to God, "I do always those things that please him" (John 8:29). That testimony and that life set Christ forever apart—unique, solitary, majestic.

The people of St. George's, Edinburgh, still talk about that memorable occasion when the saintly Alexander Whyte leaned over his pulpit at a Wednesday evening service and said earnestly to the assembled people, "This week I met the wickedest man in Edinburgh." And then to the hushed and startled congregation he whispered, "And his name is Alexander Whyte."

Believe me, that great man of God was not engaging in dramatics. He spoke what he felt in his heart because he had been living so close to his matchless and incomparable Lord. Our first step then is to admit our weaknesses as well as our strength.

Second: We shall become much more patient in bearing the faults of others when we realize there is much in ourselves that is difficult for others to endure.

One of the most searching sentences in *The Imitation of Christ* by Thomas à Kempis is this: "If thou canst not make thyself such as thou wouldst, how canst thou have another at thy pleasure? Gladly we desire to make other men perfect, but we will not amend our own fault."

I know of no better check on censoriousness, whether in the family circle, in the church, or in our social relations, than this: The moment we begin to feel indignant about the conduct of somebody else, let us stop and ask ourselves this question: "What are the things in me that are a trial to other people?"

George Santayana, the philosopher, summed up the matter when he said, "Nothing requires a rarer intellectual heroism than willingness to see one's equation written out." If we have courage enough to look honestly at ourselves, we shall be much more lenient in our judgment of others.

Third: We shall understand others better if we try to see each problem from the other person's viewpoint. Another method by which we may improve our interpersonal relations is in giving careful thought to the other person's viewpoint. A verse in the Book of Ezekiel has the prophet saying, "I sat where they sat" (3:15). Ezekiel had become exasperated with his fellow exiles in Babylon and contemptuous of them. He pronounced cynical judgments on them. Then for a whole week he lived among them, shared their difficulties, and tried to see their viewpoint. Forthwith his outlook was changed. He sat where they sat. He saw what they saw. He began to feel as they felt.

Often the key to interpersonal conflicts will be found here along with a hint as to the way they may be solved. In teenage-parental conflicts, the parent looks upon the problems of the teenager from the viewpoint of an older generation. He thinks in terms of the environment in which he himself was brought up, forgetful of the fact that in the meantime the whole social outlook may have changed as well as the physical environment. The teenager, on the other hand, looks upon the parent as someone who acts from old-fashioned, outmoded viewpoints and ideals. "Mother and Dad don't understand" is a sentence often on the lips of young people.

Husband-and-wife conflicts often develop because each refuses to see the other's viewpoint. The counselor listens to the story of the wife in which she convincingly represents herself as the innocent party. Then he talks with the husband and sees the whole affair from his standpoint. It would almost seem as if he were hearing about another home, so entirely different are the stories told. So also in employer-employee situations. It is not always easy for the employer who has lunch at his club to understand the situation of his secretary who, because of the cost, has to debate with herself as to the items she will order at the drugstore counter. Many interpersonal conflicts would be resolved if we tried to see the viewpoint of others.

Fourth: We shall discover that the highest wisdom is "Know thyself and God." "Know thyself" was the first of three exhortations inscribed on the Temple of Apollo at Delphi. This saying has been attributed to at least five well-known Greek philosophers. There is no certainty as to who originated it. Epictetus is content to say that this is "an injuction that was given to us by the ancients."

A modern thinker described this saying as "the profoundest of any two words." Certainly there is much wisdom in the exhortation "Know thyself," but it cannot stand without some qualification, for it presents an ideal that is unattainable.

Can we really know ourselves? When we make the attempt we have set out upon a task of enormous difficulty. All of us possess an almost infinite capacity for self-deception. We explain away our failures. We rationalize. We absolve ourselves of blame. We make the worse appear the better reason. We palliate our offenses, excusing ourselves and often placing the blame on others.

Thomas Nast, the American cartoonist, once attended a party with a group of friends. Someone suggested that he draw a caricature of everyone present. He did this with a few bold swift strokes of his pencil. The sketches were passed around for the guests to identify. Everyone present recognized everyone else but hardly anyone recognized the caricature of himself. This is a parable of life. All of us have a blind spot in our vision when we turn our eyes inward. Alphonse Karr asserts that every man has three characters:

1. That which he exhibits,
2. That which he has,
3. And that which he thinks he has.

Only God knows the real self, the man he is. What he thinks he is reflects the idealized image of himself. The man other people think he is is determined by the impression he makes upon them. The average person would have great difficulty in identifying these three characters. To know oneself is a hard task. It is evident, from the words of the Psalmist, that there is a wisdom greater than that of the Greeks: "Who can understand his errors? cleanse thou me from secret faults" (19:12). The Psalmist confesses that complete knowledge of oneself is beyond the power of man to achieve so he calls upon the help of God. Only God can understand him truly. Only God can free him from the blight of secret faults.

Alfred Tennyson in his poem "In Memoriam" speaks of "Working out the beast and letting the ape and tiger die," but Bishop Creighton says that after you have rid yourself of the ape and the tiger there still remains the donkey, which is a much more stubborn animal.

"Who can understand his errors?" Well, who can? Ah, yes, but we can understand other people's errors. How obvious they seem! Isn't it true that we can put our finger on the failings of even our dearest friend? Of course, we are lenient with his faults, but we are not so foolish as to suppose that he has none! Strangely enough, he may be completely unaware of the defects that to us are so plain. At the same moment, he sees blemishes in us of which we have little knowledge.

Jesus said that we can see the tiny mote or sliver in another person's eye, and yet be unaware of a beam or plank in our own. Then, rather whimsically, the Master suggests, "Wouldn't it be wiser, first of all, to remove the beam from your own eye, and then it would be so much easier to do something about the little sliver in your friend's eye."

Occasionally someone says to us, "I want you to tell me exactly what is wrong with me. Be quite honest and don't spare me." Now, let me caution that to take him at his word is to embark on a stormy sea. Few indeed are the people who can endure a recital of their defects. Of course, we can have a great time telling him off. There are few occupations more pleasurable than taking other people apart. The moment we focus our attention on the defects of others, our own self-esteem is raised and we feel superior. This enjoyable occupation is not, however, conducive to humility. The skillful spiritual counselor does not undertake to tell people their defects; rather, he teaches them the art of self-scrutiny so that they will become aware of their own failings.

James says: "Confess your faults one to another, and pray one for another" (5:16). How wise the Bible is! It gives the only basis on which it is safe to expose the faults even of a friend. The examination should be mutual, and it must be carried on in a profoundly spiritual atmosphere. Even then we shall need to keep a careful check on censoriousness and the pronouncing of judgments, and every other element of Pharisaism.

No matter how thorough our self-scrutiny may be, it is likely to remain partial and defective. We shall be either too lenient or too severe; either we let ourselves off with a superficial judgment or else we are so self-condemnatory that we are plunged into despair and feel that nothing is worthwhile. Even the judgment of a friend, while helpful, is likely to be imperfect. A friend cannot estimate how deep a longing for better things exists within us—a longing that is often frustrated and defeated. Only God's judgment is "true and righteous altogether."

The Psalmist has found the better way:

> Search me, O God, and know my heart: try me,
>   and know my thoughts:
> And see if there be any wicked way in me, and
>   lead me in the way everlasting. [139:23, 24]

The Psalmist appeals from man's judgment to God's. He knows that God's searching is not for his condemnation but for his redemption, not for his destruction but for his deliverance. The God who searches and cleanses us is the One who guides us. The divine scrutiny becomes the divine guidance.

Fifth: We shall discover that love is a healing and stabilizing force in every human relationship. Two letters came to me in one week from ministers in widely separated parts of this nation. They both asked the same question: "What should I say to parents who are greatly distressed by the unsocial behavior of their children?"

One of the ministers wrote, "There is a child in my parish five years of age who is so cruel to animals that all her pets have had to be taken from her and on several occasions she has attacked her little sister. The family doesn't know what to do." I could have stopped at that point and predicted what the balance of the letter would contain. It is a familiar and frequent pattern of behavior. She was the only child of a broken home. Then followed a second marriage that brought two little ones together in a new home. This precipitated the situation of which the minister had written. The problem presented by the second minister was identical with the first in many respects.

Now, what was the matter with this so-called problem child? She believed that she was unloved and unappreciated. This feeling of deprivation had cut the ground from under her so that she was horribly insecure and struck out blindly in all directions. Hostility and combativeness are normal responses to insecurity. This little one needed to be given appreciation and love; then a feeling of security would return and a young life would blossom forth in beauty and gentleness. Counselors often note the unintentional cruelty of parents who let a child feel unwanted, unappreciated, and, above all else, unloved.

But the need for love is not confined to children. It is universal. Maurice Maeterlinck in *The Treasures of the Humble* said, "There is no soul that does not respond to love, for the soul of man is a guest that has gone hungry these centuries back." Today the whole world is hungry for love. There is a surplus of suspicion, jealousy, and hate. Love is the only great healing force. It solves problems, comforts the lonely, and lifts men from failure and defeat to splendid success.

It is possible to develop one's power to love people, even the apparently unlovable. Thereby we manifest God and enrich our own lives. The more we seek to understand and to love others the greater becomes our capacity for receiving love. As a consequence, we draw to ourselves the love of others and this enhances our own feeling of security. Nothing makes a person more self-reliant and secure than the assurance that he is wanted and loved. Even when people feel that they are bereft of human love they will not surrender to despair if they can believe that God loves them. We can only guess at the personal tragedy that lay behind the words of the Psalmist, "When my father and my mother forsake me, then the Lord will take me up" (27:10).

I doubt if anyone will ever take the way of self-destruction who believes that there is one person who appreciates and loves him. The insecurity that leads to that dread pathway is induced, as we have seen earlier, by the belief that one is unwanted and unloved.

The greatest exponent of Christian love among New Testament writers is John the beloved disciple. On one occasion in the Ephesus Church he said to the assembled people, "Little children, love one another." From the crowd surrounding John one of the worshippers asked, "Why do you always address us with these words?"

The aged patriarch, who was the last survivor of the little band of apostles, answered, "Because it is our Lord's command and if we fulfill this alone we shall have fulfilled all things."

"There is no fear in love," wrote John in his epistle to the churches, "but perfect love casteth out fear" (I John 4:18).

Fear and love are mutually exclusive emotions. When love comes in the front door of a human life, fear flees out the back. Love is positive; fear is negative. Love is hopeful; fear is steeped in pessimism. Love is the savor of life; fear is the principle of death.

How does faith produce the love that casts out fear? First, by enabling us to believe in the trustworthiness of God. Here we find strength to meet loneliness, bereavement, disappointment, moral defeat, the desolate feeling of life's futility, or any other evil that may assail us. Right at the place of past failure victory may now be won. The testimony of the ages is that we should stake our all on the trustworthiness of God. We need only reach out a hand of faith to the Great Companion and his perfect love will cast out every fear.

The faith and love that God inspires gives us a sense of kinship with mankind. "Let us love one another," says John (4:7), and again he writes, "He that loveth not his brother whom he hath seen, how can he love God whom he hath not seen?" (4:20).

Love recognizes in every human creature a child of God. It brings a sense of belonging, a realization that in one way or another we are all bound up together in the bundle of life. These are truths that only love can teach. On this basis alone, for instance, will the race problem in America be solved. From any other viewpoint racial pride and bigotry will frustrate our best efforts to implement the Christian teaching of the dignity and worth of every human creature. Self-interest and self-love are divisive and disintegrating.

In his book, *Peace of Mind*, Rabbi Liebman says, "Next to bread, love is the food that all mortals most hunger for; it is the essential vitamin of the soul." Yet today as many people are perishing for lack of love as for lack of bread. Wherever we find a man or woman unable to give or receive love, we see one who is desperately unhappy and for whom life has lost its meaning. Without love we lose our feeling of oneness with our fellow men. Thoreau has the right of it when he says, "I call no man charitable who forgets that his barber, cook, hostler are made of the same human clay as himself." In that list Thoreau might well have included people of other races and nationalities.

In vast areas of the earth fear has replaced love. The Western nations are afraid of the Soviet Union and its satellites, and the people of Russia fear the massive power and resources of the United States; in India the Moslems fear the Hindus, and the Hindus hate and fear the Moslems; in Palestine the Jews fear the Arabs, and the Arabs fear and hate the Jews. New York papers printed a photograph of the United Nations Assembly showing the Arab and Jewish delegates seated with their backs to each other. Taut lines of hate and fear were in their faces. The United Nations, or any other political organization for that matter, can do little to remedy this situation. The will to understanding and peace must first be created in the hearts of men. Either the nations and races of mankind will learn to live together as brothers or we shall all perish.

Fear and hate are strong emotions, but love is even more powerful. Love will break down age-old prejudices and suspicions. It will foster the spirit of trust in one another. It will impel us to seek the highest interests of others as well as of ourselves.

Paul wrote to his young friend Timothy words of counsel that are highly relevant for us today: "God hath not given us the spirit of fear; but of power, and of love, and of a sound mind" (2 Tim. 1:7). In this passage Paul contrasts fear with spiritual power—love—and a sound mind. A selfish life is almost always dominated by fear. The poor little self is endangered. At any time it may be deprived of comfort or safety. As the circle of one's loyalties diminishes the intensity of selfish desires and of fears increases. The reverse of this is also true. War, despite the evils accompanying it, illustrates this fact. When I was in Britain representing American churches during the spring of 1941, I was told by Dr. Jarvis of Wellington Church, Glasgow, that he personally knew of sanitariums in both Scotland and England that had to close for lack of patients. What had cured these people, many of whom were highly neurotic? Air raids, with their ensuing opportunities to help others, cured them. Like Captain John Brown of Civil War fame, they had found a "cause." They discovered a purpose to live for. In helping others they learned to forget themselves. They had become volunteer nurses and night after night met in air-raid shelters prepared to serve the wounded when an air raid would take place.

In Central Hall, Westminster, one of London's well-known Methodist churches, I saw one such woman. In the third basement of the church was an air-raid shelter and Red Cross depot. "Notice that woman yonder, the one wearing the uniform of a volunteer nurse," Dr. Sangster, the minister, said to me. "Two years ago she was an invalid—a problem to herself and everyone else. You ought to see her when the siren sounds. Instantly she is on the job and often works all night long caring for the injured and the dying. Everyone loves her."

Here was a woman who discovered "the livability of life" when she learned how to love and serve others. She became tremendously interested in people and expressed her religious faith in a score of practical ways. No longer was she a victim of worry, self-pity, and fears for she has found that love that casts out fear.

Sixth: We shall discipline ourselves to spend time regularly each day in Bible reading and prayer. Among the great phrases that are a part of our Biblical heritage are these words that open the 40th chapter of Isaiah, "Comfort ye, comfort ye my people,

saith your God," and the chapter closes with a magnificent per-
oration on the divine power that can infuse courage and
strength into fainting hearts. The prophet makes one of the most
glorious promises of the Bible: "They that wait upon the Lord
shall renew their strength; they shall put forth pinions like
eagles; they shall run, and not be weary; and they shall walk,
and not faint" (40:31). Wait upon the unwearied God, says
Isaiah, and renew your strength. That is the central message
of this magnificent and inspiring chapter. The weakness that
waits on God is filled with divine energy.

Professor Rufus Jones, the American philosopher, once said,
"Let a person's inner being be fortified with a faith in God and
all his creative powers are quickened, his marching strength
is heightened, and his grip on everyday things is immensely increased. It is as though he has tapped a hidden reservoir of
power."

Let it be remembered that the reservoir of God's power is not
a cistern that may be depleted and drained. It is, as Jesus has
said, "a well of water springing up into everlasting life." And
that well is inexhaustible. Lake Superior, one of the largest lakes
in the world, contains 80,000 square miles of fresh water. A
child with a tin cup can no more drain its depths than can the
prayers of the whole of mankind exhaust the divine reserves of
power.

How triumphantly God's servants proclaim his availability
and his power: "My hope is in God," says one. "My strength
is in God," says another. "God shall supply all your need according to his riches in glory by Christ Jesus," writes a third (Phil.
4:19). "They that wait upon the Lord," says the prophet, "shall
renew their strength."

But how shall we draw upon these divine resources? Here are
three simple, practical suggestions:

First: *by frequent silent prayers throughout the busy*

day. This method has often been employed by some of the greatest spiritual seers of history. Ask Brother Lawrence how to draw upon God's resources and he will answer: "We should establish ourselves in a sense of God's presence, by continually conversing with him." Ask the great Horace Bushnell of Yale, and he will reply: "I fell into the habit of talking with God on every occasion. I talk myself asleep at night, and open the morning talking with him."

Second: Wait upon God by daily receiving the strength and guidance that comes from his Holy Word. We should begin the day by reading the Bible, seeking to find what God's "marching orders" are for the day. We should read until we come to a verse that speaks to our inner need, then stop and underline it. It will help if we copy the verse and carry it through the day for frequent reading. When we follow some such method of drawing upon the spiritual resources of the Bible, we never lack light on our pathway or strength for our heart.

Third: Learn to pray by communing with God from the stillness of the heart. Many devotional books, some of them classics, are available in bookstores and libraries. We need to use them as aids to prayer. As we persevere we discover that prayer is not asking favors of God but learning to live in his presence. We meditate on verses of Scripture and new insight and further vision come. We read the masters of prayer and gradually learn to pray not with words but in a shared communion. The Holy Spirit becomes a reality—"the Comforter . . . whom I will send unto you from the Father" (John 15:26).

One of the gifts of God enumerated by Paul is "a sound mind." This may be translated with equal accuracy, "self-discipline." Healthy-minded people are always self-disciplined. They have learned how to keep body and mind in subjection. They have a firm grip on their emotions. Lack of discipline over body and mind will spell future trouble.

Thomas à Kempis writes, "Who hath a stronger battle than
he who uses force to overcome himself? and that should be our
occupation, for a man to overcome himself and every day to be
stronger than himself."

No better evidence of self-discipline can be found than a devotional life that is maintained unbroken. Always there are
those who protest such a suggestion, saying, "That's too difficult
to do. My life is so full of activities and pressures that there isn't
time for a regular devotional period. In the morning I am always
in a hurry to get to work and in the evening I'm too tired."

Such a confession is an acknowledgment of an undisciplined
life. There are fourteen hundred and forty minutes in the day.
We have come to a sorry pass in our spiritual life if we cannot
dedicate at least ten or fifteen of these minutes to God. It has
been the unvarying experience of many persons that the ability
to offer a meaningful prayer from time to time in the course
of the day is dependent on their keeping inviolate a segment
of the day as a fixed time of meditation and prayer. All of us can
find time for the thing we believe to be important—and what
is more vital for our spiritual well-being than that we should
daily open "a window to the infinite"?

Nothing is so conducive to emotional stability and healthy-
mindedness as beginning the day with a brief passage of Scripture and with prayer. It sets the tone for the day, widens life's
horizons, and prevents material things and interests from closing in upon us. It inspires elevating thoughts that serve as tools
for the building of resolute character.

A professional friend of mine said recently, "I think I know
what Paul had in mind when he wrote, 'Wherefore take unto
you the whole armor of God, that ye may be able to withstand
in the evil day, and having done all, to stand' (Eph. 6:13). When
I begin the day with God, I feel like one of the knights of old as
he buckled on his armor. If I can take the hard knocks of

life a little better than some of my fellows, it is only because I have better resources with which to meet them."

There is no magic formula the repetition of which will enable us to live at our best. What is called for is spiritual discipline, fearless self-scrutiny, and the development of inner resources of courage and faith. The rewards are truly great.

LEARNING HOW TO LIVE AT OUR BEST: A SUMMATION

1. Find a worthwhile purpose in life.
2. Develop staying power to see life through to a good finish.
3. Earnestly endeavor to rid ourselves of our faults.
4. Frankly admit our own weaknesses as well as our strength.
5. Remember when we become irritated with people that there is much in ourselves that is difficult for others to endure.
6. Try to see life's problems from the other person's viewpoint as well as from our own.
7. Understand that the highest wisdom is not "Know thyself" but "Know thyself and God."
8. Never forget that love is a healing and stabilizing force in every human relationship.
9. Keep inviolate a period of each day in which to gain fresh insights into ourselves and into life and to develop the spiritual resources with which to face courageously whatever comes.

Here are fourteen points from a thoroughly tested design for living:

THE MENTAL HYGIENE CREED[3]

1. Adapt to life, immediately, completely, and gracefully.
2. Exercise, Rest, Work and Play—every day.
3. Avoid undue fatigue.
4. Discount harmful emotional urges, avoid emotional orgies, keep away from emotionally undisciplined people.
5. The five useless sentiments are: Self-pity, Suspicion, Envy,

[3] By permission of Dr. William B. Terhune, Silver Hill, Conn.

Jealousy, and Revenge. The three dependable sentiments are: Loyalty, Courage, and Kindness.

6. I shall work at a worthwhile job.

7. I face facts, discount my likes and dislikes, and cultivate an objective point of view.

8. I make clear-cut decisions and abide by them. I ask for counsel, consider it without argument, but let *no one* make up my mind for me.

9. I form good habits of living, acting, thinking, speaking and feeling.

10. I choose to see the good aspects and meanings of life. I do not deny that unfortunate facts exist and I do not overlook them, but having seen them *I choose to look for the good aspects.*

11. Knowing myself, I accept my liabilities and cultivate my assets.

12. I do not expect to get what I want in this world, and I cannot be sure I shall in the next. I will not kick against the pricks of life. I expect trouble and have accepted inevitable difficulty, that I may be free to accept opportunity unhandicapped by the sense of the difficult.

13. Fear, anxiety and worry cannot hurt me. They threaten to destroy, but they possess no weapons other than the ones I give them. Even though afraid, anxious and worried, I shall say, "Pfui, I'll get by," and continue with my normal activities, knowing that fear is the normal stimulus to courage. When the reality of courage walks with me, fear is only a shadow.

14. I believe that I am one of God's disciples; it is intended that my life have significance. God's hand is on my shoulder.

INDEX